The Golden Phoenix

Russia, Ukraine and a
Coming New World Order

JOHN HUNT PUBLISHING

First published by O-Books, 2023
O-Books is an imprint of John Hunt Publishing Ltd., 3 East St., Alresford,
Hampshire SO24 9EE, UK
office@jhpbooks.com
www.johnhuntpublishing.com
www.o-books.com

For distributor details and how to order please visit the 'Ordering' section on our website.

ISBN: 978 1 80341 275 7
978 1 80341 276 4 (ebook)
Library of Congress Control Number: 2022950703

A CIP catalogue record for this book is available from the British Library.

Design: Stuart Davies

UK: Printed and bound by CPI Group (UK) Ltd, Croydon, CR0 4YY
Printed in North America by CPI GPS partners

We operate a distinctive and ethical publishing philosophy in all areas
of our business, from our global network of authors to production and
worldwide distribution.

The Golden Phoenix

Russia, Ukraine and a
Coming New World Order

Nicholas Hagger

BOOKS

Winchester, UK
Washington, USA

Also by Nicholas Hagger

The Fire and the Stones
Selected Poems
The Universe and the Light
A White Radiance
A Mystic Way
Awakening to the Light
A Spade Fresh with Mud
Overlord, books 1–2
The Warlords
Overlord
A Smell of Leaves and Summer
Overlord, books 3–6
Overlord, books 7–9
Overlord, books 10–12
The Tragedy of Prince Tudor
The One and the Many
Wheeling Bats and a Harvest Moon
The Warm Glow of the Monastery Courtyard
The Syndicate
The Secret History of the West
The Light of Civilization
Classical Odes
Overlord, one-volume edition
Collected Poems 1958–2005
Collected Verse Plays
Collected Stories
The Secret Founding of America
The Last Tourist in Iran
The Rise and Fall of Civilizations
The New Philosophy of Universalism
The Libyan Revolution
Armageddon
The World Government

"I am not an Athenian or a Greek but a citizen of the world."

Socrates, according to Plutarch in *De Exilio* (*On Exile*).

"I was told that 22 April 2019 was a new Mayan Year of the Phoenix, which only comes round every 2,000 years. It signals the birth of a new world empire; the last time, it signalled Augustus's Roman Empire. I was told that I was bringing in a new world empire."

Nicholas Hagger, Preface to *The Golden Phoenix* , p.xvi

The front cover shows the golden-phoenix lapel badge Nicholas Hagger was awarded in Moscow (see pp.26–28). It shows a phoenix with two seven-feathered wings rising out of fire and ashes towards a halo-like sun. It symbolises a coming New World Order rising from the ashes of the Second World War and warring nation-states.

Acknowledgments

I am grateful to my PA Ingrid Kirk for her invaluable help. Without her I could not have completed this work.

CONTENTS

CONTENTS

showing section headings and structure

Preface

Russia, Ukraine, a Supranational 'Golden Phoenix' New World Order and a Coming Golden Age

A sequel to The Fall of the West *and* Peace for our Time
The Golden Phoenix follows *The Fall of the West* (2023) and at one level completes a quartet that includes *The Syndicate* (2004), *The Secret History of the West* (2005) and *The Fall of the West*. In this quartet I follow the Western *élite* mega-rich families (most notably, the Rothschild and Rockefeller families) that have controlled the West's banking, oil and natural gas behind the scenes for many decades, which Eisenhower called "the military-industrial complex" and I call "the Syndicate". The Syndicate has sought to create a New World Order since Nelson Rockefeller called for world federalism in his book *The Future of Federalism* (1962), claiming that the old order was crumbling and current events compellingly demanded "a new world order", and was quoted in *AP* on 26 July 1968 as saying that "as President he would work towards international creation of a 'new world order'".

In *The Fall of the West* I showed how the Syndicate has levelled down the West and levelled up the East to create an authoritarian New World Order, which was helped by the fact that 'Rothschilds' controlled the US Federal Reserve Bank from 1913, the Russian People's Bank from 7 November 1917 and the People's Bank of China from 1982. In *The Golden Phoenix* I carry the story forward to the Russian war in Ukraine.

The Golden Phoenix is also a sequel to *Peace for our Time* (2018), in which I described how in 2015 I was invited to Athens by a Russian, Igor Kondrashin, to attend the World Philosophical Forum's annual meeting and found myself chairing a Constitutional Convention of more than 50 international philosophers and bringing in the Russian-drafted Universal State of the Earth. I was invited to return in 2016, and Svetlana Chumakova-Izmailovskaya heard my address. I described my efforts to prevent war and bring in a universal peace.

Genesis during 2019 visit to Russia

The Golden Phoenix grew out of my visit to Russia to make a speech on 22 April 2019, which is covered in the first part of this book. I was invited for ten days (all expenses paid) to give a lecture on a supranational World State at the Civic Chamber, Moscow. My inviter was Svetlana Chumakova-Izmailovskaya, who had heard me in Athens. She was now President of the Russian Ecological Foundation, and I was told that my invitation was to celebrate my 80th birthday. In Part One I describe how before I had even set off from the UK I was sent a draft letter to Putin, which I was asked to amend; how I signed *World State* and *World Constitution* to him with peace-seeking messages (see p.31); and how I came to write him a second letter and had dealings with his assistants.

I was told that 22 April 2019 was a new Mayan Year of the Phoenix, which only comes round every 2,000 years. It signals the birth of a new world empire; the last time, it signalled Augustus's Roman Empire. I was told that I was bringing in a new world empire, which I thought would be the supranational World State of my works *The World Government, World State* and *World Constitution*, on which I was speaking.

My speech called for a supranational democratic, partly-federal World State confined to seven goals (see p.25) that would solve all the world's problems with legal powers the UN does not have. After my speech I was given the highest award the Russian Ecological Foundation could give, one of only two golden phoenixes made as lapel badges (see p.28, picture of phoenix). It was presented by a cosmonaut. The golden phoenix was originally a stamp of the Rothschild family, who had roots in Georgia, and I was told that Svetlana had taken 'Rothschilds' through four tiers of court in 2012–2013 and had won the right to have exclusive use of the golden phoenix which, in a sense, she had legally confiscated from 'Rothschilds', one of the two key families in the Syndicate. To me, learning that the new Year of the Phoenix was bringing in a new world empire and receiving the 'Rothschilds'' golden phoenix from a cosmonaut were deeply symbolic and moving.

On Tuesday 23 April 2019 Igor invited my wife Ann and me, and Svetlana and her husband, to his daughter's apartment, and Svetlana and I discussed 'Rothschilds' (see pp.34–35). Svetlana said at the end, "If you are writing a book about your visit to Russia it should be called *The Golden Phoenix*." (See p.35) Back in England I put all my Russian papers connected with my visit in a box and labelled them *The Golden Phoenix*.

Genesis after Russia's invasion of Ukraine

I was fêted in Russia and given a number of awards as Part One describes. At the end of my visit, for most of which Putin was in Vladivostok, meeting Kim Jong-un, the North-Korean leader, and then Beijing, I was invited to Putin's rest-house, the sanatorium for every Soviet leader and leader of the Russian Federation since Stalin, and given a personal concert, being sung to by two ladies in Russian dress.

Russia's invasion of Ukraine on 24 February 2022 suddenly put everything I had encountered in Russia into question. I immediately began investigating why Putin had invaded, and this is in Part Two. My renewed interest in taking up the parked title can be found in entries in my *Diary*. I wrote on 24 February 2022:

> The West is falling and Russia is getting the Soviet Empire back, reversing history after Gorbachev. And the talk of Lenin and Stalin – Putin sees himself as a successor. Ann and I were taken to Stalin's rest-house. Putin sees himself as a follower of Lenin and Stalin. The Russians now have Chernobyl, will they unleash radiation on the Ukrainians? Where does this leave Igor? ... And where does it leave me, with *World State*? The way forward... hijacked... by the Syndicate. Putin is a Syndicate creation: Rockefellers'.

I was working hard writing *The Algorithm of Creation*, setting out a first-ever Theory of Everything, and did not finish this until 25 April. I could not give the war my full attention. On 27 February I wrote:

> Caught up with the news from Ukraine, live on TV – Putin's invasion made to go more slowly than planned by fierce resistance – and in the papers: a 10-year war predicted in Eastern Europe and possibly

the use of nuclear weapons. I think of the population forecasts in *The Fall of the West* – US down to 99 million, UK down to 15 million. A Putin nuclear attack? My attempt to sit with Putin in 2019 now looks prophetic and correct. I am sorry I could not sit with him and say, "Don't do it." I nearly saw him – was taken to his health-resort where every leader since Stalin visited, and was sung to with 7 others by 2 Russian ladies.... Perhaps Putin has been misled by the Syndicate, misadvised into overreaching and having a disaster so Russia can join Europe and make a levelling of East and West possible. Emailed Lorimer, who sent me articles saying the US and Russia-China have different New World Orders. Wrote again saying the Syndicate's one will be authoritarian, the Chinese one with Russia and the West within it.

I wrote David Lorimer two emails on 27 February, first:

I am wondering if Putin has been deliberately misled by the Syndicate, misadvised with urgings to get the Soviet Union back and pushed into imperial overreach and making threats to using nuclear weapons will bring about his imminent downfall at the hands of outraged Russians, and lead to Russia joining the EU, or at any rate becoming pro-European; a drastic but necessary levelling to get the West and China into their New World Order? Time will soon tell. If not, we have ten years of war....

Secondly:

[Ned] Price [Biden's spokesman] reckons both the US and Russia/China want New World Orders. It's my contention in *The Fall of the West* that the Syndicate, which control the central banks of both sides and all the oil and gas, want an authoritarian New World Order – the Chinese one with Russia and the West in it.... A nuclear attack on the West is forecast by 2025, details are in my book along with the population in the US and UK after that.

On 28 February I wrote again to David Lorimer:

The Syndicate may have encouraged the US/EU, Russia and China to have their own separate New World Orders without sharing that these are to be combined into one authoritarian New World Order. The US may have been militarising Ukraine in preparation for their New World Order, and Russia may have been demilitarising Ukraine in preparation for its New World Order (which in their minds will get the Soviet Union back). One authoritarian New World Order cannot take place without Ukraine becoming either Western or Russian, hence China abstained. WEF [World Economic Forum] are ostensibly on the side of the US/EU, but are Syndicate with R and R ['Rothschilds' and 'Rockefellers'], who between them control Russian and Chinese finances.

When I have finished *The Algorithm of Creation*, which sets out my Theory of Everything…, I may have to do a sequel to *The Fall of the West* along the above lines: the three New World Orders, the real significance of Ukraine, and the outcome – the Great Reset into one authoritarian New World Order with the US and UK populations set to be reduced by two-thirds, and EU populations also to be reduced.

On 28 February I wrote in my *Diary*:

My thinking this morning: the Syndicate have got the US, Russia and China each pursuing its own New World Order, the plan (which they have kept quiet about) being to combine all three into one New World Order. Russia's preparation for its New World Order over 10 years was to weaken the West by getting Trump elected in 2016 and dividing Europe by refugees from Syria and by getting Brexit through by misinformation. (Johnson may now have seen that he was conned by Russian misinformation and is pro-European in his response to Ukraine, opening the UK to Ukrainian refugees, contrary to the Brexit spirit.) Deagel said 99 million and 15 million will be the populations of the US and the UK after a nuclear attack (with the EU down as well, France). If Deagel had knowledge of the Syndicate's 3 New World Order plans, the US pursued its New World Order and militarised Ukraine, Russia pursued its New World Order and needed to include Ukraine in its sphere of influence, and the

Syndicate will get Russia to nuclear-attack the US/UK/EU to get the West, Russia and China into the same New World Order. But the Syndicate's figures won't want to be exposed to a nuclear blast ('Rockefellers' and 'Rothschilds') and the Russian central bank... will not want to lose money for long during this creation of a New World Order.... Hence the initial opposition to Swift being included in sanctions. The Ukraine crisis is about reconfiguring the world order into a New World Order. This is my next work, *The Fall of the West Completed* (or *Postponed*), telling how the 3 New World Orders become one and where Ukraine was significant.

On 1 March I wrote:

Yes, there are 3 New World Orders in competition, and the Western and Russian New World Orders collide over Ukraine. An authoritarian New World Order is ahead, but the UN are distressed not to be co-operating with WEF [World Economic Forum] (the Western New World Order). There may be a nuclear war, Deagel may have foreseen this division between the West and Russia. So Ukraine may create World War 3 and 10 years' war rather than head it off.... NATO's eastward expansion, Russia's expansion into Eastern Europe and later Western Europe. Putin may fall, having been egged on by the Syndicate to self-destruct. If not, it's the fall of the West after Ukraine.

That evening was Shrove Tuesday and the annual dinner at Chigwell School (where I was once a pupil). I attended despite Covid restrictions, and when the retiring Head Michael Punt came to my table to greet me, I stood and talked to him, and he asked me what the outcome of the war in Ukraine would be. I wrote in my *Diary*:

Half-way through Punt came by.... Said in answer to his question that if Putin loses it will be the American Reset-WEF [World Economic Forum] New World Order, and if he wins it will be a Russian-Chinese New World Order.

On 2 March I wrote in my *Diary*:

> Drafted *The Golden Phoenix* and *The Golden Age*. *The Golden Phoenix* is about my visit to Russia and to Putin's rest-house, and then Ukraine. *The Golden Age* is about 3 New World Orders, Ukraine and the one New World Order, with the Golden Age of a democratic World State still out of reach. Weirdly these two books have come out of my chat with Punt yesterday, as it linked my visit to Russia to Ukraine. It was a book that spoke through me to Punt yesterday, a book I have not yet written.

In the course of March I was found to have perimyocarditis further to having mild Covid in November. I was in pain in my heart and lung area and breathless, and visited our local hospital for six days of consultations and treatments. Then an MRI showed my heart muscle was infected, and I later had tachycardia and arrhythmia and was put on beta-blockers. I was struggling to finish *The Algorithm of Creation* and I also had to read the proofs of *Fools' Gold*.

I was finally clear of *The Algorithm of Creation* on 25 April 2022. I put in my *Diary*:

> We uploaded the book and skeleton Index just before lunch. After lunch…, coming up the stairs my deep source spoke to me, to write to Dominic and mention *The Golden Phoenix*. Though pale and cold and wrapped in my stag blanket, I got out the words and sent emails…. Dominic replied that *The Golden Phoenix* should be fast-tracked and I now have to write a Proposal.

I had finally uploaded *The Algorithm of Creation* just before lunch. My "deep source", which sends me all my books, immediately switched to *The Golden Phoenix* and took me over.

My "deep source" had decided almost independently of me that I should contact my publisher regarding a book titled *The Golden Phoenix*. On 26 April 2022 my "deep source" took me over again. I wrote in my *Diary*:

While I ate a solitary breakfast my deep source poured in. *The Golden Phoenix* is a sequel to *The Fall of the West*, the one about the coming New World Orders (Western/Schwab/Agenda 2030, Russian or Chinese). Was fed the Proposal.... Went to the dentist.... Ingrid came at 10.45. Did the Proposal and Plan for *The Golden Phoenix* and sent it to Dominic after lunch.

The words were fed to me and I acted as an amanuensis and dictated them.

I was getting clear of other work. On 1 May I wrote, "Plan and do a timetable for *The Golden Phoenix*." On 4 May I had a medical day in London, during which I was able to find 80 minutes. I wrote in my *Diary*:

Back to La Brasseria [in Marylebone High Street]. Got in without a reservation, ordered yoghurt, muesli and fruit, which I made last an hour, and was there from about 11.20 to 12.40. Read the last 3 papers, and then wrote out my Plan for *The Golden Phoenix*, which represents the Syndicate. Worked it all out, Ukraine is part of establishing the Great Reset *and* keeping the oil and gas Syndicate-Russian. Was told my table was reserved for lunch and paid and left about 12.40.... The Ukraine war is about the Syndicate's oil and natural gas, and the new oil/natural gas in the Black Sea.

That evening I wrote to David Lorimer:

The West/Syndicate has succeeded in checking China's growth by its use of Covid in Wuhan in October 2019, hence China is now in lockdown. The West/Syndicate needed a Ukraine war to block Russian oil and gas that are transported to Europe via a corridor from the Black Sea through southern Ukraine (blocking which is happening throughout the EU and in the UK and US), a key plank of the Great Reset.... Putin... is threatening a nuclear strike against the UK and probably the US, and... may actually carry it out. The West/Syndicate have foreseen this and factored it in, hence Deagel. com's forecasts of massive population reductions in the West (see

The Fall of the West). The West/Syndicate's phoenix has brought us to the verge of nuclear war, and if Russia takes all southern Ukraine and takes sole control of its corridor of oil and natural gas, there may be a nuclear strike and the Russian-Chinese phoenix (an alliance) will rise at the expense of the West, with Russia looking to rule from Lisbon to Vladivostok.... That's where I am at present, waiting to hear what Putin says on 9 May.

I believe I'm... ready to start *The Golden Phoenix* about the West/Syndicate whose Rothschildian central banks will digitalise money and remove ownership as has happened in China (and partly in Russia under Lenin and Rockefellers), an important plank in the Great Reset. A nuclear strike may replace Rothschildian revolution as a way of changing the world. Incidentally I was told in Russia that the Golden Phoenix I was awarded was originally a Rothschilds badge/symbol, and that there were four court cases before the Russian Ecological Foundation won possession of it, wrested it from Rothschilds, and presented two, one to the president of Bolivia and one to me (to signify a World State rising from the ashes of the nation-states). It's a stunningly appropriate title for what's happening.

I was finally able to begin *The Golden Phoenix* in the evening of 10 May.

Visit to Russia

Viewed from the end of August 2022, the surprising thing about my visit to Russia was my involvement with Putin and his circle at a very early stage. What seemed at the time – and may still seem – a laudable attempt to involve the President of the Russian Federation in a peace plan now seems a forlorn attempt to get on the right side of a manipulative dictator who had his own agenda regarding me, perhaps associated with the Universal State of the Earth, and to get a brutal dictator who has shelled and flattened many residential areas in Ukraine to think peace. The disappearance of Lucky Lee, who interviewed me for his TV station for two hours, now seems sinister. What seemed kind and appreciative in 2019 now looks manipulative and self-interested.

I received nothing but kindness from both Igor Kondrashin, for whom I brought in a philosophical Universal State of the Earth, from his family, and from Svetlana, who awarded me my golden phoenix, and from her husband. And yet after Russia's invasion of Ukraine I was considering whether the Universal State of the Earth, and the enormous Globe Center where it was planned to be housed, were in fact aspects of the Russian New World Order, which I brought in – a New World Order that was appropriately not democratic in view of its Russian perspective, more like a New World Order designed by the Communist Party of the Soviet Union. (Igor has always been a great admirer of the writings of Engels.) And the golden phoenix I received, which then seemed so evocative in being associated with the Mayan Year of the Phoenix and with 'Rothschilds'' stamp, now looks as if it is a renewal of the Russian imperial double-headed eagle of the Tsars, twice-crowned and grasping in its claws an imperial orb and sceptre, which was on the coat of arms of the Russian Empire abolished with the Russian Revolution in 1917, to accompany the Russian New World Order. I do not believe that my golden phoenix is a coded version of this imperial eagle, but Russia's invasion of Ukraine made me stop and question everything of a positive nature I experienced in Russia.

With the hindsight of Putin's invasion of Ukraine, my letters to him and dealings with him via go-betweens look like doomed attempts to head off a ruthless Hitlerian leader from going to war, and it now seems that I was fortunate not to have been arrested like Lucky Lee, who was trying to meet me in the UK before his disappearance and was too free in his promotion of peace for Putin's liking. Moscow State University's declining to mount an event for me and the lack of contact with Putin's advisers on the last day seem to reinforce this view despite the personal concert that was put on for me in Putin's personal rest-house or sanatorium. It was as though I was half-welcome and half-unwelcome at the same time, as different factions took a supranationalist or nationalist view of me. This is the impression I have now, after Russia's invasion of Ukraine.

Ukraine

As we shall see, the main reason Putin invaded Ukraine was to follow in the footsteps of Peter the Great and take back lands that were once Russian. I see this as a consequence of a bad historical arrangement. Germany had a bad arrangement (for Germany) at the end of the First World War, and Hitler took back lands that were associated with Germany in the past: the Rhineland, Austria, the Sudetenland (northern Czechoslovakia) and Czechoslovakia before he invaded Poland allegedly to defend ethnic Germans who were being persecuted (a typically nationalist perspective). And Russia had a bad arrangement after the fall of the Soviet Union in 1991, which had led Putin to follow Hitler's example in Chechnya (always a part of Russia), Georgia, Crimea and now eastern Ukraine.

However, it cannot be denied that America had funded and armed Ukraine with a view to detaching Ukraine from Russia, and had encouraged Ukraine to join the EU before the Maidan-Square Revolution. It is also possible that up to 30 biological laboratories funded by the US were installed in different parts of Ukraine so the equivalent of gain-of-function research that was outsourced from America to Wuhan (see *The Fall of the West*, pp.67–90) could be outsourced to Ukraine. Russia's special mission was to reclaim Donbas and Luhansk from pro-Western nationalists, whom Putin described as "Fascists", but it was also to prevent Ukraine from joining NATO or the EU, and from doing experimental research on many viruses that Putin saw as a form of potential biological warfare.

According to President Biden on 21 March 2022 (see p.80), the war in Ukraine would decide who would lead a New World Order (the West or Russia-China) that would rule the world. And it is possible that Putin was challenging the West with a view to bringing about its further fall. For if, to avoid a Third World War, the West did not stop Putin from taking and retaining large tracts of Ukraine, the West's decline would be even more obvious to the whole world, and the West's power would undergo a further fall.

New World Orders

It had been apparent by the end of August 2022 that the outcome of the war in Ukraine would determine whether the Western or Russian-Chinese New World Orders would triumph and be dominant after the fighting. It was also apparent that the Western Syndicate would attempt to create an authoritarian New World Order that would include Russia and China as 'Rothschilds' owned or controlled the American, European, Russian and Chinese central banks, and 457 oil and natural-gas pipelines,[1] including pipelines across Ukraine from the Black Sea that were an issue in the war in Ukraine.

In *The Fall of the West* it looked as if the Syndicate's authoritarian New World Order was winning, and that it may have to be endured before there can be a rebellious yearning for freedom that could bring in a supranational, multipolar, democratic New World Order based on my works *The World Government*, *World State* and *World Constitution*. As we shall see, a supranational world government within a democratic partly-federal World State confined to seven goals based on my three works has unexpectedly been taken up by the World Intellectual Forum, and the supranational New World Order, in which I am now closely involved, is currently challenging the Syndicate New World Order and if there is enough support may ultimately go forward.

In *The Golden Phoenix* I describe how I was asked to sign copies of *World State* and *World Constitution* to both President Putin and President Biden; how I chaired a working group on global good governance and gave a PowerPoint presentation to India on 28 July 2022, and how on 8 September 2022 the UN General Assembly passed a Resolution to strengthen global governance; and how I was interviewed on 9 October 2022 to go out on TV to the whole of Russia, speaking on traditional Russian culture and calling for a multipolar New World Order into which Russia could move forward as an equal from the war in Ukraine, and how President Putin made a speech at the Club Valdai on 24 October 2022, speaking on traditional Russian culture and calling for a multipolar New World Order.

I would be pleased if my supranational, multipolar New World Order could happen. as I was born just over three months before the Second World War and lived through the V-1 doodle-bug and V-2 attacks on south-east England, and set myself to make the world more safe and prevent future wars from happening so that future generations of children do not have to live with the terror I had to live with of suddenly being wiped out by a flying bomb coming out of a night sky.

The Golden Phoenix and The Golden Age

So the golden phoenix I was awarded to me now stands for a coming supranational World State that has risen from the ashes of warring nation-states, a new world empire I brought in on 22 April 2019, the start of a new Mayan Year of the Phoenix that comes round every 2,000 years, in my speech that heralded in a new World State that has risen above its ecological, Rothschildian and Russian New World Order associations and now stands for the global supranational 'Golden Phoenix' New World Order. It can trump the Syndicate New World Order that will attempt to unite the Western, Russian and Chinese New World Orders in an authoritarian, dehumanising New World Order.

What will happen next, following Ukraine? My hope is that we shall see a democratic partly-federal World State confined to seven goals (see pp.151–152 in Part Three), with all nation-states remaining the same internally and (except for the seven goals) internationally, in which the West, Russia, China and the Syndicate can all participate within the overall democratic structure within the chart on p.183. The 'Golden Phoenix' New World Order is part of my legacy, a promised land that like Moses I will never live to see, and if it is implemented it will bring in a Golden Age of universal peace and prosperity throughout the world for all humankind.

12–13 July; 10, 16 August; 18 November 2022

1

Russia:
Inaugurating a New Age and World Empire

A sequel to The Fall of the West *that completes a quartet on the Syndicate*

A phoenix that rises from its ashes is a magical idea that has always had a powerful hold over human imagination. It defies the ravage of fire and is reborn from its ashes. It is like a World State rising from the ashes of nation-states ravaged by war.

In *The Fall of the West* I examined all the evidence for the origin of Covid and found its origin in gain-of-function research done within the US, and later jointly with the Wuhan Institute of Virology in China, that was funded by the Pentagon and State Department (the US Agency for International Development). The research of laboratory researchers seeking the cause of viral disease was funded by a war machine looking for potential bio-weapons.

I found that the West and the élitist Syndicate, the mega-rich dynastic families behind many world events, a network Eisenhower referred to as "the military-industrial complex",[1] was behind it. I found that the West/Syndicate were levelling down the West and levelling up the East (Russia and China) to bring about a world government in the coming decade.

The Great Reset after the pandemic, and the UN Agenda 30, in which the UN Secretary-General and the founder and executive chairman of the World Economic Forum are in partnership, would advance this program.

The Golden Phoenix is a sequel to *The Fall of the West* and completes a quartet in my study of the Syndicate, which began with *The Syndicate* (2004) and *The Secret History of the West* (2005).

I said in *The Fall of the West*[2] that the dynastic families of the Syndicate in the early 20th century were the Rothschild, Rockefeller, Schiff, Warburg, Morgan, Harriman and Milner families. To these have been added over the years the Astor, Bundy, Bush, Collins, du Pont,

Eaton, Freeman, Kennedy, Li, Onassis, Reynolds, Russell and Van Duyn families. The key families are the Rothschilds and Rockefellers, who share control of the Bilderberg Group that works behind the scenes and has been the cause of numerous world events (revolutions and wars) during the 20th century.

At this point I want to echo what I wrote in *The Syndicate*[3] as every word applies to this work:

> It is now difficult to distinguish between the individuals and their commercial firms, conglomerates of companies or corporations which shared the common interest of the Syndicate. By placing inverted commas round family names ('Rothschilds', 'Rockefellers') I seek to make clear that I am not referring to particular individuals but to a particular emphasis of a commercial pattern. When I have used, and from now on when I use, the terms 'Rothschilds' or 'Rothschildite', and 'Rockefellers' or 'Rockefellerite', I am defining an emphasis, a shade within the ethos and outlook on life of the Syndicate rather than the influence of a specific individual; in the case of the 'Rothschilds', a commercial drive associated with their 19th-century financial dominance and imperialism, and in the case of the 'Rockefellers', a commercial drive associated with their 20th-century acquisition of oil and shaping of international events through revolutions. 'Rothschildian' is a descriptive adjective meaning 'belonging to' the commercial enterprise of 'Rothschilds', as in 'Rothschildian oil interests'. 'Rockefellerite' can similarly mean 'belonging to' the commercial enterprise of 'Rockefellers'. A 'Rockefellerite' means a follower of the 'Rockefeller' faction within the Syndicate and its policies; a 'Rothschildite' means a follower of the 'Rothschild' faction within the Syndicate and its policies. 'Rockefellerite' and 'Rothschildite' mean 'pertaining to the faction and policies' of 'Rockefellers'/'Rothschilds'. (Compare 'Thatcherite', which can indicate a member of the Thatcher faction or a follower of a Thatcher policy; or even an economic or commercial direction.)
>
> In the rest of this book I am not making any imputation against the specific behaviour of any individual, family, company or corporation among the Syndicate families and their institutionalised

2

fortunes. Rather, I am presenting the achievements of the Syndicate families as part of a pattern.

I believe some of the corporate leaders and bankers among the *élite* families had a noble, altruistic vision of a unified world without war, disease or famine: of a Utopia, a Paradise. Revolutions and ideas of new world orders frequently begin with a noble aim of banishing inequality, hunger, disease and war. However, if this noble ideal was to be imposed by stealth without the consent of the people of the US, Europe and other countries of the world, then it was fundamentally undemocratic and wrong in principle, no matter how well-intentioned.

Others had an ignoble, exploitative, self-interested, capitalist vision which was to maximise their billions, turn them into more billions. To increase their profits, they desired sympathetic world leaders whose political policies would assist their commercial interests and would be happy to install puppet presidents and prime ministers who would implement their commercial policies. They would use the political situation for their own commercial ends, and were not averse to assisting both sides in a conflict if it suited them.

Each of the branches of the Syndicate have their own blend of idealism, practicality and ambition. But the different branches of the Syndicate, particularly the two factions of the Rothschilds and Rockefellers, are not really in conflict. It's more like the number-one supplier of, say, washing powder, with competing brands of its own product on the shelf. We think we have a choice, but it's offered to us by the same company. We don't realise how powerful and how connected it is because it operates in secret.

The Syndicate is fundamentally commercially motivated and self-interested in its levelling-down of the West and levelling-up of the East, as may now have become clear.

The question now is, was the Russia-Ukraine war planned as an excuse for world destabilisation that would bring the world to the brink of a Third World War and even a nuclear catastrophe, to further this program of levelling down to ashes so that, phoenix-like, a world government can rise? For the war in Ukraine is advancing one of the key goals of the Great Reset, to move away from gas (especially Russian gas) and oil to a green agenda. Was the Western Syndicate which was behind the pandemic also behind the war between Russia and Ukraine?

We shall investigate this in the second part of this book. First, I must give a full account of the invitation I received to visit Russia in April 2019, and the indirect links I had with President Putin, who is now regarded as the Hitler for our time. It was as if I had been invited to Germany in 1938 to give a lecture on world peace and had discovered that I had indirect links with Hitler. As we shall shortly see, the title of this book rose from that lecture I gave in Moscow in 2019.

*

I was invited to Moscow to give a speech on Earth Day, 22 April 2019. My invitation came from the Russian Ecological Foundation, which hosted the event in the Civic Chamber, just over two miles from the Kremlin.

Athens and the headquarters of the Supreme Council of Humanity
I have told in *Peace for our Time* (2018) how I was written to by the President of the World Philosophical Forum (WPF), Igor Kondrashin, in May 2015 and invited to the WPF's annual conference in Athens,[4] near the ruins of Plato's Academy and where Socrates said (according to Plutarch) "I am not an Athenian or a Greek, but a citizen of the world"; and how I found myself chairing the constitutional convention of the WPF, and brought in a World State, the Universal State of the Earth.[5] I have described how I was in the footsteps of the Constitutional Convention that created the United States of America in 1787.[6]

I have described how I was also made Acting Chairman of the Supreme Council of Humanity,[7] and how I returned to Athens a year later, in October 2016, and, sitting next to Igor on the platform, watched a video he played of the Supreme Council of Humanity's headquarters which had been designed by a Russian architect: the Globe Center showing the earth's continents on its outside.

4

Globe Center, from architect's video showing possible headquarters of the Universal State of the Earth and the Supreme Council of Humanity.

It was huge, larger than the Twin Towers. I was staggered and asked publicly, "When can building start?"

He replied, "Two months maybe. That will be our headquarters." He said quietly to me, "We have to decide where to put it. It could be in Athens, or perhaps Malaysia. *Your* headquarters, for you are Chairman of the Supreme Council of Humanity. You are above me. You are Head of Humanity. I want to keep a low profile. I don't want to be seen in front of what we are doing…. You and I will decide where. We may build it in Crimea." My initial thought was, 'Crimea? No way'. Putin had invaded Crimea. The world would not accept a supranational building in Crimea. I wondered if building the Globe Center was Putin's plan to win acceptance of a Russian occupation of Crimea by building a rival UN there.[8]

I have described how during that return to Athens I found Svetlana Chumakova-Izmailovskaya in the audience, of whom Igor said when I remarked, "Don't get into trouble with Putin", indicating her: "Look, Svetlana who is sitting next to Lidia [Igor's wife] is friendly with him and can visit him and explain everything we are doing…. He [Putin] knows everything we've been doing."[9] Svetlana had said she would be coming to London soon and would want to give me a present to take to the Queen.

Manila and offer of a meeting with Putin

I also told how I received the Gusi Peace Prize for Literature in Manila on 23 November 2016,[10] and was asked by a Syrian diplomat, Consul of the Syrian Arab Republic, to write a 15-point peace plan for Syria, which I was asked to take to President Assad.[11]

I have described how Igor wrote to me that Svetlana and he had "checked all possibilities for your visit to Moscow according to your Peace Plan endeavour", and that a meeting could be arranged, "maybe, even with President Putin".[12]

I was ready to fly to Lebanon and be driven across the border into Syria to meet Assad, to whom I had already signed a copy of my book *The World Government* in Manila, and the plan was that I would then leave for Moscow and perhaps meet Putin. However, on 27 January 2017 reports surfaced that Assad had had a stroke and was bedridden with a limp left hand, and it was reported that his brother was running the country while he recovered; and my visit to Syria never happened.[13]

I had said in *Peace for our Time*:[14] "I was clear that had I had an opportunity to meet Hitler in 1939 and head off the Second World War I should have jumped at the chance, or even if the outcome had been a failure, to attempt to avert the Second World War would have been a noble undertaking. And now I was in a position, as a Peace Laureate, to meet President Putin and attempt to avert a Third World War I should jump at the chance for the same reasons. I was clear that attempting to avert a Third World War, even if the attempt failed, was a noble and not an ignoble thing to do."

Invitation to Russia and draft letter to Putin

On 19 February 2019 I received an email from Igor saying that I had been appointed Universal State of the Earth Ambassador Extraordinary and Plenipotentiary, the highest diplomatic rank, and that the Russian Ecological Foundation would be holding a Forum for Mother Earth

Day (established by the UN General Assembly in 2009 as a result of a Bolivian initiative) in April, and that its president, "Mrs. Svetlana Chumakova-Izmailovskaya, whom you saw once in Athens during our annual Symposium in the past", had suggested that "the whole event" should be devoted to the celebration of my 80th birthday from 21 April, a month before my official birthday. Igor wrote that the "preliminary program is in her official letter" addressed to me, in which she invited me to "to take part in the First International Forum, 'United Earth – United Humanity – Uniform Time – Uniform Citizenship', conducted in the framework of the Global Project of the Third Millennium 'Flag of Peace goes around the World' from April 22 to April 24, 2019 in the Russian Federation, Moscow".

The draft "preliminary program with your personal participation (to be improved)" was:

On April 21, 2019 – your arrival to Moscow. Some personal meetings.

On 22 April 2019 – World Mother Earth Day – Opening of the First International Forum 'United Earth – United Humanity – Uniform Time – Uniform Citizenship' in the Public Chamber of the Russian Federation. There will be a big concert of young people from different countries.

During the whole Forum is planned the presentation of the books of the famous and prominent writer and philosopher from UK Nicholas Hagger and rewardings.

On 23 April 2019 – visit to the Red Square (centre of the whole, big Russia), also Moscow Kremlin, meeting with daughter of the first cosmonaut of the planet Yuri Gagarin; visit to the State Duma of the Russian Federation (Russian Parliament), meeting and photo with deputies (members of Parliament), visiting the Ministry of Foreign Affairs of the Russian Federation, famous Bolshoi Theatre.

On 24 April 2019 – visit to the Star City – cosmonauts' training Center in Moscow, meeting with cosmonauts, round table, awarding cosmonauts with Certificates of Citizens of the Earth, meeting with the daughter of the world famous test pilot Marina Popovich and the pilot – cosmonaut Pavel Popovich, the presentation of books by Nicholas Hagger, concert.

On 21 February I emailed Eleanor Laing, Deputy Speaker of the Commons and my MP, so she could inform the Foreign Office. There were two attachments, my intentions (see Appendix 1) and the invitation and itinerary in Russian. My email to Eleanor was as follows:

Further to my email of 3 January (below) and my wondering if Jeremy Hunt would arrange for me to meet António Guterres, I write to bring you up-to-date regarding the celebration of my 80th birthday on 22 May 2019.

First, The University of Essex, which holds my archive (and where John Bercow will be Chancellor when he retires from being Speaker), is holding an exhibition in honour of my 80th birthday in The Albert Sloman Library there. I understand there will be a rotational slide show about my 50 books and my life.

In a very recent development out of the blue, I have been invited to Moscow on 21 April 2019 for an International Forum on world unity at which my 80th birthday will be featured every day with presentations of some of my books. The program has been devised by Svetlana Chumakova-Izmaylovskaya, and I attach her letter and daily itinerary in Russian, in which my name is mentioned several times.

I repeated the program Igor had sent (see p.7) and then added:

When I met Svetlana two years ago in Athens, it was explained to me that she has regular one-to-ones with Putin, and it is not impossible that making me a figurehead in this Forum has come from Putin. If so, in view of my background in intelligence, it could be an indirect signal that Russia would like to move on after the Skripals, in which case please forward this email to Jeremy Hunt. This may not be the correct interpretation of this surprising event. There may be a Templeton explanation as I have been nominated for this year's Templeton prize, as you know. Or there may be a more simple explanation, that they need a figurehead to attract a world audience and it so happens that they have my details. But as the Putin/Skripal connection cannot be immediately ruled out, it would be wise for an expert in the Foreign Office to study this development.

Igor's last line says that I will be able to meet "somebody else… from the Russian Government", which (knowing how Igor hints, as I do) may refer to Putin. If such a meeting can be arranged, I will have an opportunity to present him with *World State* and brief him on the advantages of a new international order; and to ask him if he can arrange for me to have a meeting with Guterres.

I have replied requesting further information about the Forum, and asking if I will be able to address the Russian Parliament and meet Putin. If I do go to Russia and meet the deputies in the Russian Parliament and Putin, it will be to work for a better world for our schoolchildren and grandchildren, to remind them that a World State was called for by Truman, Einstein, Churchill, Eisenhower, Russell, Gandhi, J.F. Kennedy and Gorbachev as I said in my Gusi acceptance speech in Manila, which is in Sources on my website. As I approach 80 I am looking to move Russia and China towards a more peaceful world rather than to act punitively following what happened to the Skripals (which is a valid short-term reactive approach). As Putin is at present the biggest threat to world peace, my meeting him on my terms (if this happens) can only benefit the long-term future of the world. It is a pity that Einstein could not have had a similar meeting with Hitler in 1938.

I shall be at the gathering for Sajid Javid on Tuesday, and I wanted you to know of this development before I meet you, and him, there.

If I were to receive the Templeton prize in one of the next five years (for which my nomination is valid) I would have a platform to visit world leaders, including Guterres. I would rather Jeremy Hunt arranged for me to meet Guterres first than Putin, but I am clear that I need to get to him somehow as there is a better future for the world than the immediate disorderly future that is looming, and I need to get this across while I am still in good health.

She did not receive this email, as I established when I met her at a meeting in London involving Sajid Javid. More precisely, it was established that my email landed within the Parliamentary system, but never reached her; nor the attachment on my intentions or the invitation and itinerary in Russian. I wrote to her again, by letter this time, on 27 February:

> You did well to bring Sajid Javid to us yesterday when you and he were so busy in the House. It was a very interesting question-and-answer session, and I'm glad I raised the email I sent, which I now enclose together with the two attachments. I had an automated acknowledgement, so this email was received in the system but never reached you, and it may have been intercepted by security because of the two pages in Russian.
>
> As you will see, I have unexpectedly been invited to Russia for 21 April. It is not impossible that this invitation came directly from Putin, as the email says, and it would be wise for a Foreign Office expert to assess the situation. I am not attached to going and may not go, but if this invitation is judged to be an overture by Putin to move on after the Skripals – if he is fêting a known British intelligence agent as a way of saying sorry for what happened to the Skripals – then I should probably go.
>
> I have written to establish that I will be meeting Putin, and will keep you informed on this. It could be that they are using me for other reasons which I am still establishing, and that I should not go.
>
> It is very strange that a known British intelligence agent should be fêted in Russia for a week with high-profile visits to address the Russian Parliament, visit the Foreign Office and meet the cosmonauts at Star City. I cannot think of any other British intelligence agent who has received such an accolade on his 80th birthday. Hence my probing as to what is going on.

On 28 February I received a further email from Igor:

> The preparation of the First International Forum 'United Earth – United Humanity – Uniform Time – Uniform Citizenship' is under way.
>
> It will not be too tiring for you, because we shall have a lot of other special visits for you to the Russian Parliament, Kremlin,

Ministry of Foreign Affairs, etc, which I described already.

More detailed program will be sent to you closer to the events. You can make presentation of any of your books as many times as you like. We shall discuss this question a little bit later.

More important is that the meeting with the President Putin can happen. To make it more real, you are requested by his assistants to send him your personal letter with your request. The draft of the letter I have prepared and enclose for your approval and possibly your amendments. By return, please, send it me back to give it to Putin's office.

Another important information for you. Svetlana's Foundation would cover all your expenses on accommodation in Russia. The Hotel in the centre of Moscow will be reserved for you for two persons. So, you have only to book and buy airflight tickets to Moscow on 21 April and back from Moscow not earlier than 25 of April, and also to pay for your visas to Russia.

That is all from my side for the moment.

Waiting your approved letter to Putin as soon as possible.

So I was to meet Vladimir Putin as the founder of a World State (the Universal State of the Earth), to discuss a coming World State, and I had been requested by Putin's "assistants" to send him a personal letter and had received a draft letter to Putin to amend. I was being asked to send Putin my book *World State* and explain my supranational thinking. I was also being asked to convey Putin's personal messages to the British Government. It looked as though I was being used as a back channel.

I amended the letter Igor sent by cleaning up the English in paragraphs 1–6 and 8–10 (see letter below) without adding any ideas, and inserting most of paragraph 7. I strengthened the message of the importance of world peace and the *democratic* context of a World State by mentioning a coming "democratic, partly-federal World State", and by saying I would send him *World Constitution* as well as *World State* (not just *World State* as the short paragraph 7 said in the draft). I agreed to be a conduit between Putin and the British Government if we met. The amended letter I sent back is as follows:

"Peace cannot be achieved by force....
It can be achieved by understanding".

Albert Einstein

Mr Vladimir Putin   UK, London, February 23, 2019
President of Russia   ref. yal/sd/in – 7/2354

Dear Mr President

I have been invited to the International Forum in Moscow (which is being held in Russia from 22 to 25 of April, this year), and I wish to take this opportunity to visit you, if you are able to make time to see me.

As a philosopher and writer, I can state that all of us are living in a very tense period in the earth's history, when the whole of humanity and even life on our planet can be annihilated within a fleeting moment. It is very dangerous that most of the earth's living inhabitants and most of the world's political and economic leaders do not realise the entire seriousness of the global situation.

Some great thinkers, who have come together in the Committee of Atomic Scientists (which includes 19 Nobel Prize Laureates), try to draw attention to this. They point out that only two symbolic minutes are left until Doomsday, but very few share their justified concern.

During his time in the UN Ban Ki-moon, the former UN Secretary-General, tried to solve global problems and challenges by promoting global civil education and unified, supranational citizenship. Unfortunately, the underdeveloped consciousness of most of the current world population, including world leaders, did not support his ideas.

The World Philosophical Forum, whose Vice-President I am, is the only contemporary world entity that is continuing those ideas and plans, on the basis of classical philosophy.

Following these plans, which are reflected in the Universal Constitution of the Earth, which was adopted in 2015, the Universal State of the Earth (USE) was established along with the Supreme Council of Humanity (SCH), as a possible future successor of today's

UN Security Council. In my and my colleagues' opinion, Russia and its people, and you, Mr. President, as their political leader, could play a more significant role in creating a new, supranational global civil order, securing life on the earth, and protecting its unique nature.

If we have a chance to meet, I will present you with my books, *World State* and *World Constitution*, and will try to explain briefly the most important supranational ideas and why they are appropriate and suitable for the 21st century. As I see it, all nation-states would remain the same internally but would be linked to a democratic partly-federal World State with sufficient authority to abolish war, enforce disarmament, combat famine, disease and poverty, and solve the world's financial and environmental problems. Initially its lower house would be based in the UN General Assembly and eventually replace the UN.

We also wish to present you with the high civil-status Certificate of Citizen of the Earth-XXI – earth citizenship being the ancient great Greek philosopher Socrates' dream.

If you would like to direct any constructive ideas on international peace-making issues to the British Government or to the current UN Secretary-General, I am ready to convey your personal messages to the appropriate persons.

In accordance with The Universal Constitution of the Earth it is planned to establish an Earth Bank that will issue a universal currency, the tero. It would be nice if you could advise some financial partners from Russia to participate in this new supranational economic and financial activity.

With thanks and best wishes

Yours sincerely

Nicholas Hagger

Chairman of Supreme Council of Humanity

Philosopher, writer, WPF Vice-President,

International Gusi Peace Prize Laureate

On 7 March Igor sent a letter by Svetlana in English dated 27 February 2019, addressed to me and headed 'Invitation to Russia'. It reiterated that the Russian Ecological Foundation

> has the honour to invite you to take part in the First International
> Ecological Forum 'United Earth – United Humanity – Unified Time
> – Unified Citizenship', dedicated to the 10th anniversary of the
> International Mother Earth Day, which was established by the UN
> General Assembly in 2009 (UN Resolution No. A/RES/63/278). It is a
> very good chance to dedicate this event also to the 80th anniversary
> of your birthday, [to] the person who devoted all his life and abilities
> to describe all humans' protected future on our planet and unite
> present humanity into global citizenship, advised by the UN.
>
> The opening session of the Forum will take place on April 22, 2019
> in the Civil [elsewhere Civic] Chamber of the Russian Federation
> exactly on the International Mother Earth Day, and the whole event
> will last until April 30, 2019 at various venues.... The purpose of the
> event is a further development of the Earth's (global) civil society
> and civil diplomacy, a reminder that despite social, cultural and
> national differences, we are all children of the Earth, our common
> home which must be cherished and loved.

With it was a letter by Svetlana in both English and Russian to the Russian Embassy in London, requesting that it should help me obtain a visa.

Fast-tracked visas

The Russian Embassy visa agency VFS Global advised that we must attend in person and bring a hotel voucher and confirmation email from the hotel, and that we could not apply for a visa until we had done this. I emailed Igor, who replied that Svetlana had found a way through. I was to complete a form he sent for me and for Ann, and he would then send me a new "visa support", and I could then go to the Consulate of the Russian Embassy in London, a route for diplomats only, not the visa agency, and receive a visa within two days, not four weeks. I could then show my real program rather than pretend I was a tourist without a program. I should stay until 30 April as the Consulate preferred that length of time.

This is what happened. Igor sent me four documents to take to the

Consulate of the Russian Embassy, and on 15 March I rang and found they were closed for lunch from 12 to 2 whereas VFS Global was open until 3. We went there. There was a photo booth near the entrance for taking photos in the correct size, and a fingerprinting machine on the counter. The queue was not too bad, and our passports were taken and returned to us by courier on 21 March containing Russian visas for 15 days.

We could now book our airline tickets with British Airways, to arrive at Moscow Sheremetyevo airport at 16.50 on Sunday 21 April. Meanwhile at Igor's request I attached a short biography and nine photos. Igor sent an announcement in Russian about my coming speech in the Civic Chamber on 22 April.

Letter from the UK Foreign Office Minister of State responsible for relations with Russia

On 26 March Eleanor Laing emailed me a letter from Sir Alan Duncan, the Minister of State who was in charge of Russia at the Foreign Office, dated 20 March. I received it on 28 March. Its gist was that normal relations had been suspended following the Novochoking and attempted murder of the Skripals, and that I would be visiting Russia in a personal capacity:

> Thank you for your letter of 4 March to the Foreign Secretary, on behalf of your constituent, Mr Nicholas Hagger about Russia. I am replying as Minister responsible for our relations with Russia.
>
> The current planned high-level bilateral contact with Russia has been suspended but we continue, where necessary and possible, to speak to Russia diplomatically and culturally. As the Prime Minister has repeatedly said, we have no quarrel with the Russian people.
>
> As a fellow Permanent Member of the UN Security Council, we will continue to engage Russia on topics of international peace and security. We will also use these channels of communication to make clear there can be no place in any civilised international order for the kind of barbaric activity which we saw in Salisbury in March 2018.
>
> I met First Deputy Foreign Minister Titov on 16 February in the margins of the Munich Security Conference and sent a clear message that Russia needs to choose a different path before there can be

any change in our relationship. Russia must act as a responsible international partner.

Please assure Mr Hagger we will continue to sustain and build people-to-people relations including through culture, education, science, sport and tourism. We will also continue to mark our shared history, as we did at the Armistice Centenary commemorations in November 2018. Building these relations at a time of political tensions matters, as it will help expose the Russian people to UK ideas and values and encourage them to work with the UK in the long-term.

Please thank Mr Hagger for his offer of assistance, however, in any meetings with Russian Government officials, he is acting in a personal capacity.

Requested to bring greetings from Prince Charles

I had been asked at an early stage if I would bring greetings to the Russian Ecological Foundation from Prince Charles, as my masque *King Charles the Wise* had come out the previous November. On 8 March I wrote to Prince Charles's Assistant Private Secretary, and on 25 March received a reply from the office of the Prince of Wales:

I am grateful to you for taking the trouble to write as you did, but I am afraid His Royal Highness is unable to do as you ask. I am sorry to send you such a disappointing reply, but trust that you understand. This letter comes with The Prince of Wales's best wishes.

On 28 March I wrote to the office of the Prince of Wales:

I have kept the Foreign & Commonwealth Office informed from the outset so there could be an informed decision, and on 26 March received a lengthy letter from Sir Alan Duncan from the Foreign & Commonwealth Office's short-term policy on Russia, and I am not surprised.

I was asked by the Foundation that invited me if I could bring greetings from His Royal Highness to the opening ceremony, where (it now transpires) I am to speak for 15 minutes as "special guest" before all the ambassadors to the countries in the Russian Federation (see enclosed Civic Chamber announcement of my visit). I felt duty-bound to ask, but do understand the Foreign & Commonwealth Office's sensitivities regarding Russia at present.

I see it as my duty to go and fulfil the program and do what I can to improve long-term relations with Russia, which may be using me as a backchannel. I have been told that I may be discussing the dangers of war with President Putin, and in my view it is in the long-term interests of the UK, the Commonwealth and the peace of the entire world that this sort of conversation should take place.

Please convey my very best wishes to His Royal Highness.

The reply from his office on 16 April 2019 seemed to confirm that Prince Charles could not formally send greetings to the conference because of the Foreign Office's strictures:

I am writing to thank you for your letter and enclosure of 28 March conveying your good wishes to the Prince of Wales.

It was most kind of you to take the trouble to write as you did, and this letter comes with best wishes.

Now I knew I was not bringing greetings from Prince Charles, on 16 April I emailed my speech to Igor so it could be translated into Russian for the interpreter. I told Igor there was no more I could do. I had in all honesty and openness kept both sides informed. I was allowed to make a visit at a personal level but must not represent the UK (as would greetings from Prince Charles).

Russian announcement of speech

On 18–19 April the semi-governmental Civic Chamber of the Russian Federation, which had been created so prominent citizens could interact with the Russian government there with Commissions being involved, now announced my speech on its website in Russian. Translated into English the announcement was as follows:

Special guest – British writer Nicholas Hagger
April 22 at 18.00 in the Public [better translation, Civic] Chamber of

the Russian Federation (Miussakaya square, 7) in the framework of the global project of the 3rd millennium 'The Banner of the World Goes Around the World', the opening of the 1 International Forum 'One Earth – one mankind – one time – one citizenship'. The forum is dedicated to the 10th anniversary of the International Day of Mother Earth, established by the UN General Assembly in 2009 on the initiative of the plurinational state of Bolivia.

The special guest of the forum is the world-famous British writer, historian, philosopher, laureate of the international peace prize Gusi [better translation, Gusi Peace Prize] Nicholas Hagger. Hagger's books are read by the leaders of many countries and members of royal families. All his life he devoted [to] the idea of uniting humanity into a single global citizenship and protecting the future of all people on our planet. During the event there will be a presentation of Hagger books.

The organisers are the National Ecological Fund [better translation, Russian Ecological Foundation], the Commission of the Russian Federation on the development of public diplomacy, humanitarian cooperation and the preservation of traditional values.

Event moderator – chairman of the Commission Public [better translation, Civic] Chamber, Elena Sutormina.

Representatives of civil society from more than 30 countries, ambassadors, employees of embassies accredited in the Russian Federation, the Russian Foreign Ministry, the UN Information Center, UNESCO, the GPA, the WFF, Russian and Soviet cosmonauts, scientists and cultural workers will attend the opening of the forum.

I was a "special guest" and much was made of my Universalism and of my work to unite "humanity into a single global citizenship".

The goal of the conference was to save Mother Earth from wars and climate change. Igor asked me to prepare a 15-minute-long speech for the opening ceremony. I included images that could appear in a presentation on a screen behind me. He said that in Moscow he would ask for a text with slides marked for the interpreter. Each sentence I spoke would be interpreted into Russian and the interpreter would need to know where to pause. Igor said he had not received the program as certain things were still being "fixed"; he wrote, "So many people want to meet you that you could stay here for one or two months." He asked me to bring 15–20 copies of *World State* and be ready to explain the main ideas at a number of venues.

In the days before I went to Russia, with my PA I transferred images onto pen drives as optional background for any speeches I would have to make.

Now all I had to do was to travel to Russia and deliver my speech, and then handle what would follow.

Arrival in Moscow

At Moscow's Sheremetyevo airport Ann and I were met by Slava, Igor's son-in-law, who was very amiable and friendly and made it clear that he did not work but helped Igor full-time. He told me he was reading one of my books in Russian. He wheeled our luggage to Igor's battered car. I shook hands with Igor and he embraced me.

Slava drove us. I did not realise he had obscured his number plate so he would not be recognised on the automated system and charged for parking at the airport, and a couple of miles down the road we were stopped by the police. Igor got out and talked with them, and the police left. I began to realise the authority he somehow had with Russian officialdom.

Greeting at the hotel

Slava drove us to the Beta Hotel. Svetlana greeted us in a formal line with two of her four grandchildren, all in Russian dress, and gave us a loaf and salt, a traditional Russian way of expressing hospitality and welcoming family members and friends. Her grandson was holding an accordion, her granddaughter flowers, which she presented to Ann. We were then shown up to our room by Slava, room 2211 on the 22nd floor, and twenty minutes later we all met in the restaurant for chicken wings and liver pâté, and Russian borsch soup with beetroot – not Ukrainian borscht, Igor said with some pride; and later fruit and a yoghurt. Igor said that his wife Lidia was at their house in Greece, but I would be meeting his daughter Natasha and her son from her previous family.

Igor said that 350 wanted to attend the opening ceremony in the Civic Chamber, but the hall only held 250, so 100 had to be turned away.

Difficulties following the Novochoking of the Skripals

Igor said, "Just as the Foreign Office did not allow greetings from Prince Charles, so here we are not allowed things to do with you." He said that our visit to Moscow State University had been cancelled. "The visit to the Kremlin is still on." Gorbachev was very ill but we were to visit his Centre and I could leave a book for him. "Putin is in a corner from other world leaders and is reacting defensively and aggressively." I suspected I would not be seeing Putin. The program after my speech was still not fully known. "They are weighing requests and we make decisions each day." He said of the daughter of cosmonaut Yuri Gagarin, "Gagarin's daughter is abroad, but you can leave a book for her." The Russian Academy of Sciences was not meeting until May, and I should leave a speech for someone to read.

Then Igor said, "This hotel was built for the Olympics in 1980. You are the first British to stay here, the first in nearly 40 years."

Monday 22 April 2019: cultural centre

That night we slept over eight hours. We breakfasted and relaxed until 12. I put on the suit and tie I would be wearing at the opening ceremony. We were being shown some of Moscow on our way to my evening lecture.

Igor came, and Slava drove us to a cultural "palace" built around 1980 that displayed Russian crafts. It was arranged as shops. We went into a shop that sold plasticine historical figures, and a marzipan shop, where the English-speaking manager told me, "Russia is again an empire," meaning that it had ethnic minorities. I told him Russia had left its union stage (the Soviet Union, its stage 43 of its 61 stages) for its federation stage (stage 46), a decline, and he said "Toynbee". In fact it was not Toynbee who saw civilisations as passing through 61 stages that included a union that eventually gives way to a federation, but me in *The Fire and the Stones*, part later updated as *The Rise and Fall of Civilizations*. I told him Toynbee got Russia wrong, it's a Byzantine-Russian civilisation that continued the Byzantine Orthodox faith.

The KGB

Slava drove us on. He passed the Kremlin and Igor pointed out the KGB building and said enigmatically, "You'd better watch out, Nicholas", and I wondered whether he knew of my work for British Intelligence from 1969 to 1973.

The last time but one we were in Russia, in October 1995, we flew to Yalta, and at the end of our flight back to Moscow's Vnukovo airport our plane was boarded by two ladies in military uniform with peaked caps who lined all passengers in one line in the aisle, and Ann and me in another line by ourselves. They confiscated our passports and left the plane.

It took us an hour to retrieve our passports. We wandered about in the airport, hearing the name "Hagger" being broadcast in Russian, and up to the first floor. Ann found a loo and disappeared behind the door, and a Russian lady in military uniform rushed forward and banged on the door and shouted in English, "KGB toilet, not for you." She took us to where our passports were left.

The KGB had taken our passports. She returned them, but the very fact we had been singled out suggested the KGB was still aware of what I used to do, and were letting us know.

As soon as we reached our hotel room that day in 1995, the phone rang and a Mrs. Bankhoul was telling me: "Aleksandr Solzhenitsyn asked me to ring you. He cannot see you as he is not in Moscow." His biographer had given me Mrs. Bankhoul's address and I had written offering to bring Solzhenitsyn four of my books. The next morning, by arrangement with Mrs. Bankhoul, I took them to Solzhenitsyn's apartment.[15]

We passed the Hotel Ukraina, where I stayed during my visit to Moscow in 1966. I recalled the food being served there in one go, all the courses together, and a box lift with no front door. We passed the office where Igor worked. It was next to the Foreign Office. He was not forthcoming about the work he did there, so close to the Foreign Office. I recorded, "The seven Stalin-style buildings."

We stopped for a view of Moscow near the Moscow State University, which was not hosting us now. At the station Slava left to pick up Igor's wife and take her home.

Civic Chamber

Igor drove us to the Civic Chamber. We stood beneath the phoenix of the Russian Ecological Foundation, and then went up in the lift. A Russian Colonel greeted us in uniform, and was photographed with us.

The Civic Chamber was a wide room with sloping seats, and a huge screen at the front on a raised stage. The audience was coming in. A lot were standing, chatting, some were sitting in comfortable seats. I was shown to the front seat by the aisle with Ann and was photographed and videoed. An Admiral came by in uniform, Admiral V.A. Popovich, and gave me a book he had written in Russian: *Na Opasnom Rubyezhye* (Moscow, 2018), *At the Dangerous Edge*. It had a picture of an atomic bomb mushroom cloud exploding over a devastated city on the front cover and a quotation from Karl Marx on the title page. There were many coloured pictures at the back, one of which (the caption said) seemed to show the crew of the *Moskva* in 2017. He had already signed his book to me. He said in Russian (Igor told me), "You are my best friend." A Vice-Admiral sat behind me. Many of the audience came and shook my hand, and some wanted a photo.

Then Svetlana appeared. She was working hard on the order of the events and we had a short chat. She told me that 22 April 2019 was the start of the new Mayan Year of the Phoenix, which comes round every 2,000 years and heralds a world empire (the last one being Augustus's Roman Empire). Then she was off talking to groups of participants at the side of the stage.

The formalities began. There were speeches in Russian. An Indian lady from New Delhi, Purnima Anand, spoke. A Russian "translator" interpreted to the hall. A speaker reminded us that it was Lenin's 149th birthday that day. I whispered of Lenin to Igor, who was sitting next to me, "He would have come up with a central plan to sort out the world," and Igor agreed. He whispered, "He wanted a United States of the World," and, "You sound as if you're a Communist, like me." I whispered, "Yes," and immediately realised I should have whispered, "Universalist", for Lenin was a Universalist.

A South Korean spoke in Russian very animatedly. I was told he owned a TV station, and was known as 'Lucky Lee'. He hogged the lectern and would not stop. Igor was no.14 to speak. Two or three others spoke after him. I was no.24 on the Russian program, but was suddenly announced at about no.18 as some speakers could not be called because the South Korean had overrun.

Speech

I stood at the lectern and noticed a number were in military uniform. I spoke before the screen, which showed 13 images to illustrate what I was saying. The "translator" interpreted for the Russian audience and there was a pause each time he stopped.

He referred to me as "Your Excellency" as I was the Universal State of the Earth's Ambassador Extraordinary and Plenipotentiary and the Chairman of the Supreme Council of Humanity, roles clearly accepted by the audience. I fleetingly half-wondered if the Universal State of the Earth, along with the Globe Center, were part of a Russian program to bring in a *Russian* World State, to be called the Universal State of the Earth, at the beginning of a new Year of the Phoenix.

Nicholas Hagger making his speech with the interpreter standing beside him and the cameraman who followed and filmed him throughout his visit.

There was lengthy applause when (on my personal initiative following the Foreign Office's letter) my opening words described the UK as "Russia's wartime ally". In my speech I said:

Distinguished Ambassadors and guests, ladies and gentlemen, I bring you greetings from the United Kingdom, Russia's wartime ally. I am very happy to be here for Earth Day, which is focusing on climate change, plastic pollution, protecting endangered species and the environmental movement.

One Earth, one mankind. The cosmonauts with us have seen the Earth as a ball and, looking from space, must have found it hard to believe that sustainability and pollution are such serious problems in such a beautiful planet, and that such a beautiful planet can be riven by wars.

As a boy of four I lived in Churchill's constituency, which the Nazis bombed every night. There is a picture of me taken in March 1944, aged four, after Nazi bombs blew out our windows. I'm holding a piece of glass. I lay awake at night listening for flying bombs (which we called "doodle-bugs"). When they cut out I would count up to 10, and there was a big bang, and I was relieved it had not fallen on our house. Ever since then I have dreamt of a world of peace in which small boys will not lie awake at night listening for bombs.

Since 1945 there have been 162 wars the UN was unable to prevent and the UN is currently struggling to keep the peace in 73 of them, which are still continuing. When I was a boy of four there were no nuclear weapons and now there are 14,900, and one day terrorists will steal one. One Earth, one mankind – the ecology is very important, sustainability and climate change. But behind these, helping these, is the movement to abolish war and work for disarmament and create a world free from war, a united world, a united Earth.

You may be interested to know that I first had the vision of a united world here in Moscow in 1966. I was a Professor in Japan for four years, and I travelled back on leave from Japan to London via Moscow, and I went to the Cathedral of the Archangel and had a vision I put in my poem 'Archangel' – nearly 53 years ago. Since then I have had 50 books published within literature, philosophy, history, international politics and statecraft and other disciplines, and I am very pleased to be back at the source of my vision of a united world.

Earth Day. In my philosophy I've developed Universalism which presents the whole of humankind's relationship to the Earth, and the universe, through all disciplines. Universalism sees the Earth as a whole and each human's relationship to the Earth and the universe. On the cover of my book *The New Philosophy of Universalism* is an image of the expanding universe with a surfer on the edge in a cosmonaut's helmet. This is showing what happens on the edge of the expanding universe. The universe is surrounded by the infinite and the surfer's feet are in space-time but the rest of him is in the infinite. This surfer is also an image for Earth Day, humankind as a cosmonaut in relation to the Earth, seeing the Earth as a whole, as a united world.

During this Forum in the coming days I shall be talking about how to bring universal peace to the world to underpin our focus on ecology and combat the effects of climate change. I shall be talking in particular about two of my 50 books, *World State* and *World Constitution*. After the first two atomic bombs in 1945 there were calls for a democratic World State from President Truman, Churchill and Einstein, who were all shocked by the news, and the tradition continued with Eisenhower, Russell, Gandhi, J.F. Kennedy and Russia's own Mikhail Gorbachev. I called for a World State when I received the Gusi Peace Prize in Manila in 2016.

In my book *World State* I've continued the tradition and I've worked out some details and I'll be talking in greater length about this later in the Forum, a way of getting a peaceful world that can do all the things that ecologists need to happen, that can implement improvements throughout the world. All nation-states will remain the same internally but they will support a limited federation with sufficient authority to bring world peace in seven areas: to abolish war and enforce disarmament, combat famine, disease and poverty, and solve the world's resources and environmental problems. It would initially be based in the UN General Assembly. There would be no arms race, saving nearly two trillion dollars a year (that's 2,000 billion dollars). The arms race is a waste of everybody's money. The Earth movement will benefit from this dividend.

Earth Day calls for the world's leaders to solve climate change, end plastic pollution, protect endangered species and broaden the environmental movement across the globe. It's about the enduring health of Mother Earth, for environmental protection and the unity of humankind: one global citizenship in a world of peace. In 2015 I was pleased to chair the Constitutional Convention that brought in the Universal State of Earth, which promotes global citizenship. All problems could be solved if the world can live in the context of universal peace, in which war is made illegal.

Earth Day and the Earth Movement bring an optimistic attitude to the world's future. The 19th-century English poet Tennyson wrote 'Ulysses' in 1833 and it was published in 1842. The elderly Ulysses leaves his kingdom in Ithaca to his son Telemachus and sets sail for new adventures. The ecology movement on Earth Day can take something from his optimistic attitude, which through my World State I share. Towards the end of the poem Ulysses urges his crew:

> Come, my friends,
> 'Tis not too late to seek a newer world....

He's old, but he's seeking to bring in a newer world. The last lines of the poem are:

> Tho' much is taken, much abides; and tho'
> We are not now that strength which in old days
> Moved earth and heaven, that which we are, we are;
> One equal temper of heroic hearts,
> Made weak by time and fate, but strong in will
> To strive, to seek, to find, and not to yield.

That's how we should be, strong in will, to seek and find a new world, a World State in which all the world's environmental problems can be solved by a central plan.

Thank you and happy Earth Day, everybody.

Award of a Golden Phoenix

There was lengthy applause and I returned to my seat, but was recalled. I was presented with an award by the Russian Ecological Foundation. The presenter was a cosmonaut, Aleksandr Lazutkin, who wore a ribbon with a medal shaped like a star, a 'Hero of Russia' medal.

Nicholas Hagger unexpectedly receiving the Golden Phoenix from cosmonaut Aleksandr Lazutkin, with an explanation by the interpreter and on the screen (above), and then reacting (see below).

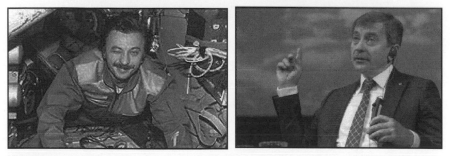

Aleksandr Lazutkin as a cosmonaut in 1997 (left) and in 2015 (right).

I later found out he had spent 184 days in space in 1997 as flight engineer on the Soyuz TM-25 mission to the Mir space station. He has said in interviews that one views the earth differently from space, there seems to be harmony between nations which is absent on earth.

He shook my hand and gave me a lapel stud or badge of a phoenix rising, in pure gold, the Order of the Golden Phoenix, to mark my inauguration of a new age of world peace on the first day of the Year of the Phoenix, which was bringing in a new world empire. I tried to get to grips with something extraordinary that seemed to have happened: my golden phoenix announced that I had brought in a new age of world peace and a new world empire on the first day of the new Year of the Phoenix. The phoenix was the logo of the Russian Ecological Movement, and a leather booklet of notification accompanied my award. It had a golden phoenix on the front cover and inside, and there was a blue stamp of a golden phoenix over which there were two signatures (one Svetlana's).

The phoenix was referred to as a "golden phoenix", but on closer inspection it is in white gold with the base of its body in yellow gold,

The Golden Phoenix lapel badge.

like the rest of the yellow lapel badge. The white gold was to make it stand out from its yellow background. White gold is an alloy containing 75 per-cent gold and 25 per-cent nickel and zinc.

The Golden Phoenix commemorates the first cosmonaut, Yuri Gagarin, who rose from the ashes of the Second World War into space like a phoenix rising; hence Igor's wanting me to leave a copy of *World State* for Gagarin's daughter. It is a gold "breastplate" or badge of a golden phoenix, shaped like a drop of water which is crucial to life and symbolises the ecological universe.

The Golden Phoenix also symbolises humankind's physical and metaphysical presence in the universe. It shows a phoenix rising within the Fire of eternal life, its head haloed by the sun (the Light), its wings shaped like a bowl to receive inspiration from the wind in the air, and the rays of the Light. Each wing comprises seven feathers, which can be seen as the seven main disciplines and the seven branches of literature. The phoenix also symbolises the World State rising from the ashes of the devastation of nation-states at the end of the Second World War.

The Golden Phoenix is the Russian Ecological Foundation's highest award. I was later told by Svetlana that only two copies of the golden phoenix had been made, by someone I would be meeting. One had been given to the President of Bolivia for getting Mother Earth Day established with the UN General Assembly. I was given the other for my Universalist approach to a World State and lifelong work for the unity of humankind. Svetlana said: "The Golden Phoenix is rising from the ashes." And I saw it as a symbol of the unity of all nations in a World State, with the ashes being nation-states. I said this to Svetlana, and she nodded.

Then she said it was originally a Rothschilds symbol. There had been four court cases, and the Russian Ecological Foundation had been awarded the right to use the image of the Golden Phoenix. So I had been presented with a Rothschilds image. My book *The Syndicate*, which is about an *élite* (mainly the Rothschild and Rockefeller families), had been translated into Russian and (I was told) was widely read – and was being read by Slava when I arrived in Moscow. I had been presented with an award that, like a vortex, set off a whirlpool-like rush of many associations that included being the stamp of the 'Rothschildian' Syndicate and the Golden Phoenix of the Syndicate's coming New World Order.

So the Golden Phoenix was a symbol for: the Western US-based New World Order risen from the ashes of devastated nation-states after the Second World War; the Western Syndicate's New World Order risen from the ashes of the levelled-down West and levelled-up East; my democratic World State that included all nation-states, on which I had just spoken; and a Russian New World Order risen from the ashes of the Soviet Empire devastated by Gorbachev's changes – a possibility that until then I had barely considered.

In the course of expressing my thanks, improvising, I called for an improvement in long-term relations between Russia and the West, and there was lengthy applause.

Award of the BRICS silver medal

Then I was presented by the Indian lady from New Delhi, Purnima Anand, President of the BRICS International Forum and International Federation of Indo-Russian Youth Clubs, with the BRICS octagonal silver medal on a ribbon with the British (and Russian) colours of red, white and blue. On the back it said 'Vision for Future' and 'New Delhi, India'. BRICS stands for Brazil, Russia, India, China and South Africa, and the decision to award me this medal was made in consultation with all these countries. The lady from New Delhi was representing these countries. I had been honoured by both Russia and India.

Holding hands with a Russian Admiral and Vice-Admiral on stage

Then there was a concert, with Russia's ethnic minorities taking part in music and dancing. At the end I was summoned to the stage and found myself between the Admiral and Vice-Admiral, both in uniform, the Admiral, Admiral Popovich, with many coloured ribbons and medals. They each seized one of my wrists, and I thought, 'I've said too much near the Kremlin, I'm being arrested.' But they raised my arms in a 'V for Victory' sign, and I was on the internet holding hands with a Russian Admiral and Vice-Admiral.

There was a song, and then, still on the stage, I was interviewed in a mêlée and was asked several questions. In reply to one question about Putin in relation to a World State, I said Putin could explore, and organise a report on, a World State, and go to the Secretary-General of the UN. I said I would offer my services to help this. Many wanted photos with me. I wanted to speak to the cosmonaut who awarded me the Golden Phoenix about his seeing the unity and harmony of the earth from space, but he had quietly slipped away.

I was approached by an ex-MP, and the interpreter said he would arrange for me to meet MPs in the Russian Parliament. The South Korean known as 'Lucky Lee' asked to interview me at his TV station for half an hour about my books and find common ground with his movement. Svetlana carried me away, clutching at my sleeve, for photos on a different floor. Igor was in our picture, holding the ball of the earth in his hand.

After a swirling series of meetings Igor drove us back with the South-Russian Head of several universities. She said she would invite me to address the students. We arrived back at the hotel, too late to eat, having also missed lunch. (Instead of lunch we had had "honey mead" in the wooden cultural "shopping centre".)

It was now 12.45am. I felt I had begun to turn Russia round, open the way for an improvement in its long-term relations with the West.

Signing books for Putin

The next morning, Tuesday 23 April, we were to go to the Russian Academy of Natural Sciences. I breakfasted at 9.30 and then walked to a nearby bank and changed £100 for 8,050 roubles. I returned, and, at Svetlana's request the day before, reinforced by Igor, signed two books to Putin: *World State*, on the title page of which I wrote "For President Vladimir Putin, Hoping you will set up a working party to explore taking the world into a democratic World State with a universal peace, with my best wishes, Nicholas Hagger"; and *World Constitution*, on the title page of which I wrote "For President Vladimir Putin, Hoping a working party can explore a World Constitution that can be laid before the delegates of the UN, with best wishes, Nicholas Hagger".

I had been told I should carry these with me and have them ready as there would be an opportunity for one of Putin's assistants to give them to Putin.

We had coffee and an apple strudel (early lunch), and Igor came about 1.30. We picked up Svetlana, who was waiting on a street corner. In the car I told her I had signed the books, and there was a discussion of the plan for me to visit Putin. I said I would like him to get me to the UN. Svetlana said I should see Putin and give the books to him myself rather than via an intermediary.

Russian Academy of Natural Sciences

We reached the Russian Academy of Natural Sciences and were

shown into a small room where half a dozen Russian professors, the top six academics, sat with Lida Ivanitskaya, the Vice-President of the Academy. She stood and made a long formal statement, welcoming us. Then I made a statement, showing *The New Philosophy of Universalism*, and talked about my Universalism, my surfer on the crest of the wave of the expanding universe with his feet in space-time and the rest of him in the infinite. I talked of my ecology, and my *World State* and *World Constitution*, which put my thinking into practice.

The professors discussed what I had said, in English. They liked it, they said it accorded with their view of globalism. I said, "You are Universalists." I said that I went to Sartre's front door in Paris in 1959 to learn about Existentialism, and now they had come to me to learn about Universalism. I said Lenin wanted a United States of the World and was a Universalist without knowing it. A man who identified himself as a journalist asked me about Syria. I said I had been asked to conduct a peace mission there in 2016, but it did not happen. There was a heated digression on Napoleon. Why had the UK not entered Paris in 1812 while Napoleon was involved in Russia?

Then Lida stood and made a speech to camera saying that my ideas on Universalism had such quality that she would submit my three books (*The New Philosophy of Universalism*, *World State* and *World Constitution*) for a prize that had recently been won by a Chilean. And she presented me with the Academy's silver medal showing a bespectacled Vladimir Vernadsky (1863–1945), a mineralogist and geochemist who founded geochemistry, biogeochemistry and radiogeology. The medal was attached to a silver bar that contained a ribbon with white, blue and red stripes (Russia's colours). I thanked her and handed her copies of the three books.

Anton Antonov, one of the professors, said he was in charge of 80 within the Russian Academy of Natural Sciences, and he asked if I would work with them. And a philosopher and ecologist, Igor Riurikk-Ternov, asked if I would work with him on the Vatican, and make a return visit to Moscow for a discussion. I said that if I were invited I would return to Moscow.

I was asked to fill in a form by Lida, the Vice-President of the Russian Academy of Natural Sciences. It was connected with the prize she wanted to enter me for. Igor Riurikk-Ternov, a member of the Union of Russian Writers, sat alongside me filling in a similar form, I understood to support my nomination for the prize. I never discovered what prize I had been entered for.

Nicholas Hagger completing a form alongside
Igor Riurikk-Ternov, being filmed by the cameraman.

Nicholas Hagger about to be interviewed for a film, with
Igor Kondrashin (left) waiting to interpret, with an image of
Vladimir Vernadsky on the wall (see p.32).

A film about my call for world peace

Then a film camera appeared and everyone made themselves scarce, and I was interviewed in the same room on my own for a film about the most important men who are contributing to peace. I had to make two statements to camera, and Igor interpreted. The film-maker (who had long hair to below both jaws) had filmed my speech and the activities in the Civic Chamber, and told me the film will be mainly about me: my coming to Moscow and calling for world peace. He said he would be following the rest of my visit and would be with us every day.

Igor 2 and Putin

All of a sudden there was a heated discussion between Igor and Svetlana on one side, and Igor Riurikk-Ternov (Igor 2) on the other side, voices were raised. Igor and Svetlana later explained to me they were arguing against his nationalism and urging him to recommend me to an assistant to Putin who was then in China, whom he knew well. They said I had to go to the Union of Russian Writers the next day as the Russian Academy of Natural Sciences had asked me to work with the Union of Russian Writers, and Igor 2 would be present. I should write a letter to Putin as soon as possible in case it was needed to accompany the two books I had signed to him.

Svetlana and Rothschilds

We were then driven with Svetlana to Igor's daughter Natasha's and her husband Slava's very modern apartment and were served sparkling Russian wine. Svetlana asked me about the Rothschilds, and also the Rockefellers (who had been deeply involved in Russian life since they funded Stalin's five-year plans from 1925), and having explained how the families worked together and in conflict with each other at the same time, I went on to talk about how Stalin's daughter Svetlana Stalin had approached me in May 1996 and how I talked with her for five hours in Cornwall, and she was not aware that her father had a link with Rockefellers.[16]

In the course of the evening, Svetlana told me more about the Golden Phoenix. The first golden-phoenix lapel badge was made in March 2016 on the international day of water as a gift for the President of Bolivia, whose country set up Mother Earth Day. It was shaped like a drop of water, the water of life, and showed a phoenix rising from ashes that were dowsed and dampened by water.

The second golden phoenix was made for 22 April 2019, for me.

It has a diamond within the pure gold which came from Yakutia in Siberia. To me, the diamond symbolised the Light the soul can see within its body's distractions (which I had talked about in Athens in 2016). The last Year of the Phoenix brought in the Roman Empire's rule of the world, and now the phoenix of world government had again risen from the ashes.

Svetlana said that the ancient Greeks and Egyptians described a mythical bird, called a phoenix, that lived for 500 years. She said, "The phoenix was based on the sva, a bird in Yemen. Rothschilds wanted the phoenix so they could use it as their stamp, and they stole the idea from Russia in 1988. I took them to court from 2012 to 2013 and won it back, with no costs, after going through four tiers of the court. So I have the right to put it on the Russian Ecological Foundation's letter-heading as its logo."

She added, "The phoenix is thought to have originated in Georgia [the former Soviet republic], and a Georgian gave me the stamp. The Rothschilds were from Georgia and had relatives there and used the phoenix as a stamp in the 1770s, and took it again in 1988. It was in Mexico before then, but used by the Rothschilds."

I thought, 'So it's an anti-Rothschilds image, and if Prince Charles knew about the court case, it may have been a factor in his not sending greetings.'

Then Svetlana said: "If you are writing a book about your visit to Russia, it should be called *The Golden Phoenix*."

And I knew I had a sequel to *Peace for our Time*, about the inauguration of a new age and world empire, and the rising phoenix of a world government.

Second letter to Putin
We got back to our hotel room at 1.35am and I had to draft a second letter to Putin to accompany the two books I had already signed to him. I worked on it till 2.40am and only had five hours' sleep.

The next morning, Wednesday 24 April, I sat in a business computer room on the hotel's ground floor and, allowed to use the business computer there, finished keying in my letter to Putin within an hour. Igor read it later and made some amendments. Then I did another hour, printed it off and got it saved on a memory stick. The letter, which then joined the two books to be given to an assistant to Putin, was as follows:

Moscow, 29 April 2019, TS
To Vladimir Putin

Dear President Putin,

As the author of 50 books I was invited to Russia by the President of the Russian Ecological Foundation, Svetlana Chumakova-Izmailovskaya, to be their special guest at the international forum for Mother Earth day in the Civic Chamber in Moscow on 22 April. I said I brought greetings from the UK, Russia's wartime ally.

In my speech I described my new philosophy of Universalism as a philosophy of the whole of humankind. I said that solving the earth's ecological problems is difficult under the present system, and that I can see a democratic World State ahead, as called for by many thinkers over the centuries from Plato and Kant to Truman, Einstein, Churchill and Eisenhower. I have worked out the details of such a democratic global State in two recent books, which I have pleasure in enclosing and have signed to you: *World State* and *World Constitution*.

All nation-states would remain the same internally but would allow a supranationalist federal democratically-elected world Parliament to abolish war, control disarmament, solve famine, disease and poverty and environmental problems such as climate change and energy resources. This world Parliament would start in a limited way for perhaps one day a month at the UN General Assembly to save expense. It would be a World Parliamentary Assembly of 850 seats, I give the constituencies in *World State*. The arms race would end and the peace dividend could be around 2,000 billion dollars a year, which could be spent on lifting the living standards of the peoples of the world and solving ecological problems.

I have some following as having chaired the constitutional convention that brought in the Universal State of Earth in 2015, and as Chairman of the Supreme Council of Humanity. In the UK I am in touch with Prince Charles of the royal family, whose assistant sent me best wishes before I left on Sunday, and I am concerned to see an improvement in relations between Russia and the Western nations....

I would like to visit Antonio Guterres at the UN and ask him to set up a working party to explore the idea of transitioning the UN into a World State over a period of time. I would like to give a presentation on this subject to the UN delegates. I would appreciate an influential letter of introduction to Guterres that will guarantee my being given an appointment. I would then like to meet someone in the US Government, preferably President Trump. I see a revival of the wartime alliance of the UK, USA and Russia. Next February will see the 75th anniversary of the Yalta conference, when Churchill, Roosevelt and Stalin met. I wrote an epic poem *Overlord* nearly 25 years ago about the end of the Second World War, and visited Yalta to do research, and as Chairman of the Supreme Council of Humanity would be happy to host or take part in a ceremony at Yalta in the Crimea, and hope that you can be present.

There is a plan to improve relations between Russia and the West at a time when a new generation is emerging, and I can be an Ambassador in this respect. I need something new to happen, which I can report to Prince Charles and inform the UK Foreign Office. I would be grateful if you could spare time to meet me any time you consider possible.

I can see benefits in the world perception of you if you could agree to set up a working party to explore my pioneering view of a World State, which carries forward a long tradition and which this week has resulted in awards to me by the Russian Ecological Foundation (a pure-gold phoenix), BRICS (a medal for vision of the future), and the Russian Academy of Natural Sciences (who gave me a medal and have asked me to work with them and with the National Union of Russian Writers).

Svetlana Chumakova-Izmailovskaya has organised my program, and you may like to make an arrangement through her. My email address is at the top of this letter. I understand that some of those around you will want to focus on the negative European and world situation now rather than on the prospects for improvement, but I believe you have vision and I would be very grateful if you could see fit to see me so I can convey a message that may transform

Western-Russian relations in the coming months and years, to the benefit of all humankind in accordance with the principles of political Universalism. Lenin, a Universalist who wanted a United States of the World, would be very interested in my initiative.

With best wishes, Nicholas Hagger

Writer, philosopher,

Chairman of the Supreme Council of Humanity

Gorbachev's consultant

We then drove to the Gorbachev Foundation. There was a gold plaque outside. We went up in the lift. Vladimir Polyakov received us, consultant to Gorbachev and his International and Media Press Secretary, a quietly spoken man with excellent English. The fellow who was filming me was not admitted as Svetlana had not given the Foundation his name. He filmed us outside at the end.

I sat with Vladimir, Igor, Svetlana and Ann and made a statement about what I was trying to do, how I was continuing the tradition of calling for global governance or a World State, and how I would like to improve relations with Russia.

Vladimir told me that Gorbachev was in hospital but not seriously ill, he was still writing at 88, his latest book was called *Towards a New Civilisation*. He said Gorbachev might see me later in my visit, after looking at the copies of *World State* and *World Constitution* I had signed to him, and Gorbachev might write to Guterres at the UN on my behalf.

Vladimir said, "He is very concerned that his changing of the world has evaporated, and the Cold War is back." He said, "If you are seeking to speak with Putin you are on your own." He made it clear there was no relationship between Putin and Gorbachev. He said, "There were 69,000 nuclear weapons and he and the US President cut them back [to the then current 14,900]." He made it clear that Gorbachev was on my side, and Putin probably wasn't. (Igor cut Gorbachev out of my letter to Putin as, he later said, Putin was jealous of Gorbachev's reputation and publicity.)

We spent half an hour talking with Vladimir and looking at the pictures on his walls, and then went down to the second floor and looked at Gorbachev's books, awards and certificates, which were behind glass as if in a museum.

We then went on a long round trip of Moscow. It was during this drive that, with Igor and Svetlana sitting in the front of Igor's car and the conversation having turned to oligarchs, I asked, "Is Svetlana an oligarch?"

"Yes," Igor replied emphatically.

Svetlana added, "Yes, I am an oligarch."

Nicholas Hagger, Svetlana Chumakova-Izmailovskaya and Igor Kondrashin holding banners of the Golden Phoenix and Triple Code (see p.48) at the Gorbachev Foundation near a picture of Gorbachev on the wall.

We passed the Kremlin and ended at a metro station. We took the metro to the Kremlin and walked to where the tanks drive past the mausoleum (then under scaffolding and closed) where Putin would stand for the victory parade to celebrate the Russian victory in the Second World War on 9 May. The tanks would keep within a pair of yellow lines painted on the cobbles, which would guide them. The Lenin Museum, where I queued and saw Lenin's body in 1966, had been turned into a museum on the Napoleonic Wars of 1812.

A Georgian phoenix-maker in Red Square
In Red Square we encountered (presumably by arrangement rather

than accident) the Georgian who saw the phoenix in a vision in Mexico in 1989 (he told me in Russian with Igor translating), and produced the two designs for the two golden phoenixes given to the President of Bolivia and to me. He said it was Svetlana who found out about the Year of the Phoenix being 2,000 years old in the Mayan calendar; and that he did not know about Rothschilds, Svetlana did. She wanted the phoenix to be her logo, and Rothschilds had stolen the copyright, he said. Svetlana was clearly a forceful oligarch, taking on the might of Rothschilds and winning.

After a walk along the Kremlin walls we returned on the crowded metro. Igor tapped a man in a seat on his shoulder, and he gave up his seat to Ann. On the way back Igor told me that his daughter Natasha, who worked in a Swiss bank, earned a lot of money and owned the apartment we had visited without a mortgage, and that his wife Lidia lived in a *dacha* (second home) ten miles outside Moscow, which was a base for their children. They had a house in Sochi (which is associated with international winter sports), and another in Greece. He said he occupied a house of Natasha's, and that all the houses were bank-funded.

Television interview with Lucky Lee

The next morning, Thursday 25 April, Igor and Svetlana came at 11am and drove us to the South-Korean Lucky Lee's television studio. He was a showman. He wore a scarf over his back saying "Make peace, not love". He showed me a picture of himself with more than 20 chorus girls in Times Square, New York, and complained that the US had blocked his request for visas for them to make a return visit. He took me to a room with two armchairs, and interviewed me in English. An interpreter translated my answers into Russian.

A dozen sat round in the darkness, including Igor and Svetlana. Lucky Lee's first question was, "Do you really like Russia?" I talked of Russia's having been the UK's wartime ally, and about my appreciation of Russia's 19th-century literature, of Dostoevsky, Turgenev and Tolstoy.

The interview went on and on. The half hour originally requested turned out to be two hours. I was asked many questions and was able to talk about the World State I envisage, peace, going to Guterres at the UN, wanting an introduction to him, and so on. I came up spontaneously with a couple of new ideas: there should be a huge Universalist conference hosted and paid for by Russian oligarchs for nation-states to sign treaties that they will not attack each other, in preparation for their disarming; and that there should be a conference to put Universalism on all university syllabuses and to fund films. I spoke like the Chairman of the Supreme Council of Humanity they expected me to be.

At the end there was food in an adjoining room: segments of fruit and chocolate biscuits. Lucky Lee told me he would now make a short film of our interview, and in a week's time send it to all TV channels in the world; and he would make a long film to go to all world leaders and send it to them after two weeks. He would be sending this long film to Guterres, Trump and Putin. He said, "You may become Putin's world-peace adviser."

Then his "twice ex-bride" – he had married and divorced her twice – came in, a high-wire artist. He stood up and kissed her, and she went and sat next to Ann and talked with her for the rest of the time we were there. We left about 3pm.

Lucky Lee arrested and imprisoned

So far as I am aware, the two films never happened. In late July 2019 Lucky Lee tried to come to London to meet me. He was stuck in Amsterdam and his flight was delayed. When he arrived I was on my way to Cornwall and missed him.

On 29 August I heard from Pavel Pestov, one of his staff, that Lucky Lee had been arrested in Crimea for "biting a policeman's hand" at a demonstration. He asked if I would publicise his case.

On 24 August Lucky Lee took part in the Tavrida-Art Festival, a youth festival in Crimea that was attended by 92,000. A man, introducing himself as the organiser, began to prevent amateur filming that had allegedly been organised by Lucky Lee. Lucky Lee called the police, who instead of solving the dispute, arrested him. Lucky Lee was accused of biting the hand of a police officer, and was detained in Sudak, Crimea "for 10 days". On 26 August he was transferred to

Simferopol detention centre in Crimea, known to be one of the most overcrowded prisons in the Russian prison system, with conditions compared to torture.

In a statement available online,[17] Lucky Lee said that at 10pm on 24 August, the day of his arrest, he began a hunger strike. Since this communication nothing has been heard of Lucky Lee.

Svetlana said he had promised to send her his film of an interview with me, but he never sent it, and so far as I am aware he has disappeared.

Lucky Lee was clearly identified with calling for peace in Crimea. I wondered if a faction within Russia wanted to put an end to the two films he was making about me that would spread the idea of a democratic World State round the world, and, alarmed by his visit to London, had taken him out.

Moscow branch of the Union of Russian Writers
We were driven to the Moscow branch of the Union of Russian Writers. It had been founded in 1830 but was in a nearby building until 1953. I entered a room that had a 1953 feel about it, where I was aware Boris Pasternak and Aleksandr Solzhenitsyn had sat. I sat next to Wladimir Boyazinov, the head of the Moscow branch of the Union of Russian Writers, at a polished table. Igor 2, who seemed to have requested this visit, sat the other side of me.

Wladimir gave us a talk about the history of the Union of Russian Writers, and then I began an account of my works, and of *World State*. Igor 2's phone rang, and he left the room to take the call. He returned giving a thumbs-up to Igor. He announced that Putin's assistant (over whom Igor and Svetlana, and he, fell out at the Russian Academy of Natural Sciences) was in China with Putin, but his deputy would be joining us.

He came in, a balding Armenian dressed in black, and presented me with an anthology of poems that included one of his own. Igor 2 had another phone call. He returned and announced that Putin's assistant in China would be back on Sunday and would be with us on Monday, when I would hand over the copies of *World State* and *World Constitution* I had signed to Putin, and my letter to Putin.

I was then made a member of the Union of Russian Writers and received a badge of a rippling flag in the Russian colours of white, blue and red. I was asked if I would help them, and I said I would, which gave Wladimir "hope". We then had to leave abruptly before I could finish my account of my books.

Somehow the main purpose of the meeting had been to connect me, as a member of the Union of Russian Writers, to Putin's assistant in China via his deputy.

Signing books for Igor and Svetlana

Outside Igor said there had been a change of plan. We had been going to an art exhibition, but instead we should return and eat and then Igor 2 would join us. This clearly had something to do with Putin.

We returned to our hotel, and around 8pm, at their request, I wrote messages in copies of *World State* and *World Constitution* to Igor and Svetlana. Aware that these might be shown to Putin, I signed *World State* to Igor as my "fellow supranationalist and deviser of the Universal State of the Earth and the Supreme Council of Humanity, this book about the concept of a World State, with thanks for all the organising of our program and tireless driving, with affection and best wishes, Nicholas Hagger"; and *World Constitution*, "For Igor Kondrashin, who has himself written a constitution, with thanks for

Nicholas Hagger handing signed copies of World State and World Constitution to Igor Kondrashin and Svetlana Chumakova-Izmailovskaya in the foyer of the Beta Hotel, Moscow.

many discussions on a World State and World Constitution, with best wishes and in admiration of your vision which can see a future structure of the world and your way of getting it across, Nicholas Hagger".

I signed *World State* "For Svetlana Chumakova-Izmailovskaya, with thanks for organising a wonderful program from 21 to 30 April 2019, and for presenting me with the Golden Phoenix, and with best wishes for the success of the Russian Ecological Foundation, with affection and best wishes, Nicholas Hagger"; and *World Constitution*, "For Svetlana Chumakova-Izmailovskaya, who has vision and can see the future structure of the world, with best wishes, Nicholas Hagger".

I handed Igor and Svetlana their books in the hotel foyer.

Igor 2 a General, on closed space

We ate upstairs, and about 9.30pm Igor and Svetlana said to Ann that she could go up to our room, so she went. Igor 2 arrived around 10.15pm, with ice-creams for all. We went to the café and ate our ice-creams. Svetlana did not want hers, so I took two up to Ann (who was lying on her bed, watching TV). I returned downstairs, and the real discussion began.

With Igor interpreting, Igor 2 said he had written a book, *The True Construction of the World*. He said he had met the Pope (Benedict XVI) in 2012 to tell him something, but that Pope did not last long: he resigned soon afterwards. (He was replaced by Pope Francis.) I now grasped why he had asked at the Russian Academy of Natural Sciences if I would help him work with the Vatican.

On a sheet of paper Igor 2 drew a circle round a saucer that was on the table (and had held the ice-creams) to represent the earth, and marked the spot outside the circle where all cosmonauts have reached and, having left a gap, drew a downward line where the cosmos begins. He said a cosmonaut has never reached the cosmos where space begins, just some ten times higher than I was with British Airways. And that the cosmos cannot be entered. He was saying that no cosmonaut had reached the moon.

I said, "A cosmonaut who has gone to the moon would see the earth as a ball."

44

Igor 2 agreed. He said, "But no one has any moon dust."

I said, "Ann has two moon rocks I gave her, which allegedly came from the moon."

Igor 2 said, "The earth is covered with clouds. Space is closed and cannot be entered."

He then showed his identity card. Igor studied the card and said to me, "He is a General of the Ministry of Extraordinary Experiences."

I thought of UFOs, and extraordinarily wild theories.

Igor 2, the General, said: "Space is closed, so no one can come to us, but there are other worlds like ours that are not seen by us."

Igor, interpreting, said, "It's like the planetarium. You see the stars on a ceiling. You can't go beyond the ceiling."

I showed the expanding universe on the cover of *The New Philosophy of Universalism* and said I had spoken to Einstein's assistant, David Bohm, who confirmed that Einstein would be happy with my view of the universe. The General said, "There are no nuclear weapons. North Korea has the only one."

I detected misinformation, and said I had spoken to Hiroshima survivors in Japan and was satisfied the two atomic explosions had happened.

The General said, "Nuclear arms are a business, that's why Syria happened, to sell arms." He added that his work draws on the "Triple Code", the three-circle triangular image (see p.48) on Notre-Dame (see p.49), under the tower of Oxford University's St Mary the Virgin (see p.50), and on the Kremlin's Cathedral of the Archangel (see **p.54**). He presumably meant that each of the three circles is separated from the others by space.

Svetlana said that in the Civic Chamber I had signed the Roerich Declaration like Roosevelt, protecting the culture of the UK, the US and Russia. (I had thought I was signing a visitors' book as having been present.) She said the symbol of the Roerich Declaration is also the Triple Code.

The General said he did not want to go to the Vatican again as last time the Pope only lasted weeks. He wanted to give his book to me to publish under my name. He said I should take it to the Queen as it would change everything.

Igor said, "There will be no cost to you, only cost this end."

The General's book: closed space and no nuclear weapons except in North Korea

After questioning, the General said he had been working with a group from the Russian Academy of Sciences (which is more prestigious than the Russian Academy of Natural Sciences) and the Union of Russian Writers, and I would be "top of the group" and listed with the others on a plaque. He said, "The book I will give you will be as significant as Copernicus and Galileo, it will change everything." He declined to say in what way, but I already had a good idea of what he meant.

I asked what I would tell the Queen: "Would it be, 'Here is the basis for a universal peace, we are separate from the cosmos and must live at peace, this will bring Russia close to the West'?"

Igor agreed.

The General said, "It is difficult, I know what's in the book but I can't say. It's difficult for Nicholas to understand now, but all will become clear when he receives the book. It will lead to universal peace and he will be credited with it."

I reflected on what he had said: space is closed, so no Americans have been to the moon, all moon landings have been faked. No cosmonaut has been in space, so Yuri Gagarin was faking. There are no nuclear weapons except in North Korea, so Hiroshima was a fake, as was the Cuban missile crisis. Even if the earth is surrounded by closed space it would not follow there would be universal peace. It needed Putin to help with that.

Igor asked if I could now leave so they could stay and have a short chat in Russian. It was 11.45pm and I said I had to go to bed and went upstairs. Ann had waited up for me.

Later I reflected, 'So I am to be given extraordinary knowledge that will spread my books round the earth, and I have to take a book to the Queen.' I recalled that Svetlana had wanted me to take a present she would give me to the Queen in 2016. Perhaps she wanted to give me the book, which had been shown to the Pope in 2012. I had been chosen to convey a present to the Queen then, in 2016, and I had been chosen again now, in 2019, even though (as the Foreign Office letter had explained) there was no relationship between the UK and Russia.

I *was* being used as a back channel as I suspected. The film interview now looked like a put-up job to interview me for two hours on my suitability for this knowledge.

I was to be enrolled in the very prestigious Russian Academy of Sciences. I had championed a Renaissance outlook – the unity of the universe and humankind – in many disciplines in my works, and with hindsight my talk at the Russian Academy of Natural Sciences had been perfectly judged.

I could not help wondering if this was an attempt to discredit me, to challenge my Universalism and democratic World State by getting me to put my name to ideas that were unproved and mad (closed space making journeys to the moon impossible, and the only nuclear weapons produced by North Korea). This could be an attempt to bring my international reputation into disrepute to stop me advocating universal peace. In view of what later happened to Lucky Lee, who may similarly have been discredited, this was a possibility I could not ignore.

Tree-planting

The next day, Friday 26 April, Igor and Svetlana came for us at 10.30am and drove us to a suburb of Moscow where I was to plant a cedar from Siberia. It was in a public garden surrounded by relatively recent houses. The cedar looked like a fir and was very green. A gardener stood by to help me with a spade.

I was greeted by a member of the Mayor's department who held a mobile phone and took photos and then interviewed me, holding his phone towards my mouth with Igor translating, for the local news, which was on Moscow television after the national news. I was asked about the Golden Phoenix I had received, and a coming Universal State 2,000 years after the Roman Empire.

The Mayor's representative showed me a certificate saying I had planted the first of 193 trees of peace that would be planted in all the UN's nation-states, the first of a million ordered by the Siberian Mayor. I made a short speech: "I am happy to plant this tree, which symbolises a new era of universal peace that begins now." I was told that a plaque with gold lettering would soon be on a wall in Moscow to commemorate the event. The only others there apart from the Mayor's representative were Svetlana, Igor and Ann. But my tree-planting, filmed on the Mayor's representative's phone, apparently got on Moscow's television news that evening.

I then heard that Trump had called for the US, Russia and China to get rid of their nuclear weapons. In my speech on 22 April, I called for an end to the 14,900 nuclear weapons as a terrorist might steal one. I half-wondered whether Trump was following up my call for a united earth in Moscow on Mother Earth Day.

The Triple Code

We went on to a restaurant called 'Chocolate Café' and Svetlana ordered several courses for a communal lunch: soup, salad, chicken, vegetables, éclairs, ice-cream, green tea and later cappuccino. Igor told us that Gorbachev was now very ill in hospital, his health had deteriorated and he would not be able to see me.

Then Svetlana gave me a maroon-and-white lapel badge of the Triple Code: three small circles set in triangular form on a white background within a larger circle (see picture below).

Lapel badge showing the Triple Code,
given to Nicholas Hagger in Moscow.

We discussed the Triple Code at some length. It is very old and seems to have originated in Yemen (Aden), which also had a variant of the phoenix, the sva, as we have seen (on p.35). The Triple-Code symbol was probably brought to England by Crusaders; but it is found in every culture, including the Chinese and Mongolian cultures. In China it is in the separation of Heaven, Earth and Man, and also in *yin*, *yang* and the *Tao*. The Triple Code is also in Islamic art. As the Triple Code Model of numerical cognition, it embodies three primary representational codes or numbers: Arab digits, verbal number comparison and non-symbolic magnitude comparison. And so it was at the heart of medieval Arab maths. It has also been claimed to be in the separation in medieval Christian theology of Heaven, Earth and Hell.

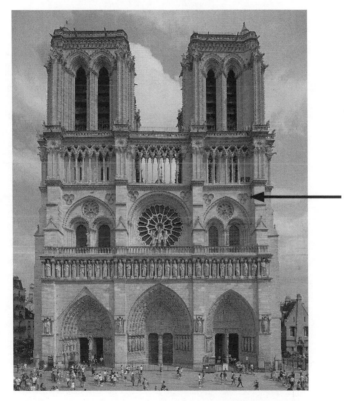

The west façade of Notre-Dame showing six Triple Codes as upside-down triangles in a row (arrowed), three on each side of the 1225 west rose window, which is on the cover of Nicholas Hagger's *The Fire and the Stones*.

Crusaders may have seen it in Muslim and Christian art and brought it, perhaps from Yemen or from a derivative culture to key ecclesiastical buildings: to Paris (Notre-Dame, which has six Triple Codes on its west front, three on either side of the 1225 west rose window which is on the cover of my book *The Fire and the Stones*, see below); to Oxford (the University church of St Mary the Virgin, Oxford University's first building and the seat of its government, used

Oxford University's church of St Mary the Virgin on the north side of the High Street with stone tracery round stained glass showing the Triple Code (arrowed), dating back to at least 1252, under the 13th-century tower (see below).

for lectures and the awarding of degrees from at least 1252, with the Triple Code in the stone tracery round stained glass under the 13th-century tower, see above); and to Moscow (the Kremlin's Cathedral of the Archangel, built between 1505 and 1508 on the site of an older cathedral built in 1333, with the Triple Code on a façade, see p.54). It may originally have consisted of three stones to denote a sheikh's house. Svetlana was in touch with 100 sheikhs, and the most recent one sent me his best wishes via her.

Moscow City Duma

We left at 5pm and drove to the Moscow City Duma (Council), and hung around in the garden until 6.30pm, admission time. We were not on a list and had no seat reservations, but eventually got in. There was a reception in progress to celebrate 25 years of the new Duma since 1993, and I had some champagne.

We had a tour up the stairs (chandeliers and pictures) until we reached the Great Hall, which was the English Club in in the 1820s and 1830s and still had an English feel.

There we attended an event. We sat in comfortable seats a few rows back from the stage. There were five presentations to the Diplomatic Club of the Duma, all associated with the Foreign Office, and then two singers and a pianist sang and played to us.

At the end I walked up onto the stage and shook hands with the tall Chairman of the Moscow City Duma, Alexey Shaposhnikov, who was in a suit. I had a long chat with him, and photographers and a man with a television camera appeared, and seeing our conversation as an important moment and egged on by Svetlana, filmed us. I was told we would be on the main Moscow news later that evening. Alexey told me he met Prince Charles during the Moscow Olympics and asked me to convey his best wishes. I presented him with a copy of *World State* under the noses of two dozen members of the Foreign Office who were standing round. The Foreign Office, like Moscow State University, had declined to see me.

We had a final piece of cake (chocolate and fruit) downstairs, then we left to take the metro home. We changed at a station that had statues of revolutionaries crouching under the arches with weapons, and got out at Partizanskaya, the station for our Beta Hotel with statues of partisans between the tops of two escalators.

"Colonel Igor" and a blocked book

The next day, Saturday 27 April, I breakfasted and then had half an hour on the hotel's business computer to write a letter to Elena Gagarina, cosmonaut Yuri Gagarin's daughter, to accompany the book I was leaving for her. I then had coffee downstairs in the café with Ann.

Igor crept up on us and announced himself saying, "I am invisible, I know how to move invisibly." I knew he had graduated at the Moscow State Institute of International Relations (now MGIMO), which was under the umbrella of the Russian Foreign Office and whose alumni included the Minister of Foreign Affairs, Sergei Lavrov, and many of Russia's ambassadors, and I jokingly called him, "Colonel Igor". He smiled.

We set off with him for the metro. As we walked there was talk of how we were getting nearer Putin, who had been away, meeting the North-Korean leader at Vladivostok, and then in China. He said we were going to the State Duma (the Russian Federation's Parliament) on Monday to meet a party leader who knows him. Igor said I was to say that Trump's call to Russia and China to get rid of nuclear weapons and then saying he wanted to withdraw from the global arms-control agreement (the Intermediate-Range Nuclear Forces Treaty) signed by Reagan and Gorbachev had left us confused. He said I could go to Guterres and find out from the US what is happening.

On the metro he also let drop that the General had rung him throughout the event in the Moscow City Duma, but he had blocked his (the General's) calls. He rang Igor before he got home and spoke to him for an hour, saying he wanted to work with me and send me the "closed room" information – that the earth is like a closed room in relation to space – in *The True Construction of the World*, and also offered alternative routes to Putin.

The next day when we were in the car I raised the General's book, *The True Construction of the World*. Igor and Svetlana said they had seen it, and had decided it was not worthy of being sent to me.

Sergey

We got out at a station and went up to the street, and there stood a man in white shirt and white trousers. Igor said, "Svetlana's husband." He added that Svetlana was staying at home and working on getting me to the State Duma on Monday, making many phone calls; and that Sergey would be looking after us.

We had encountered him briefly in the hotel foyer on the first day, he was supervising their grandchildren. He took pictures of me at Dostoevsky's statue and we walked to the Kremlin. He ran off to get tickets to go to the Cathedral of the Archangel, where I had first glimpsed world unity in 1966, and to the Diamond Depository, which was presided over by Elena Gagarina, Yuri Gagarin's daughter.

The Cathedral of the Archangel

We then queued up steps to get into the Kremlin's inner grounds. We walked past the old Congress Hall, and the Tsar's cannon and bell, to the Cathedral of the Archangel. It was a white building with impressive golden domes.

It was very dark inside, but once our eyes got accustomed to the darkness I was full of wonder again, 53 years after I was last there, at the Tsars and saints with gold haloes round their heads, and the second icon to the right of the altar of the Archangel Michael, where I had my vision of world unity in 1966, totally unchanged. The Archangel Michael was guarding the Gates of Paradise and calling for a new universal age of peace. I recalled the vision I had of the end of the Cold War and of a World-Lord. I put my vision in my poem on Communism, 'Archangel':

> As I stared at the murals' centre
> In this Cathedral-tomb,
> The Archangel became a Shadow
> With a sword and wings outstretched,
> And I saw in the second icon
> The future of the West,
> From the Atlantic to the Urals:
> Into the People's Square,
> From the Cathedral gates,
> File in the morning rush-hour
> An *élite* of self-made Saints

Each still on the last hour's quest....
Decades of contemplation
Show in their white-haired peace
As, trusting to perfect feelings,
They value each equal they greet;
Until, whispering on silence,
They glide to the Leaders' Hall,
Their hearts, with a World-Lord's wholeness,
At the centre of life, of all,
Their hearts where all past and future meet.[18]

I had seen the 'World-Lord' ruling the world in a wise collective leadership of gentle people who lived by universal – indeed, Universalist – values in a reunified Europe in which the Cold War, and all wars, had ended.

We were not allowed to take pictures but Igor seemed to have the authority to overrule this ban, and we openly took several. Afterwards we went outside and found the Triple Code at the top of a façade (see immediately below). Sergey took a picture of me with the façade in the background.

A façade of the Cathedral of the Archangel
showing the Triple Code at its top with
Nicholas Hagger beneath.

The Diamond Depository

We then walked down to Stalin's part of the Kremlin and joined the queue for the Diamond Depository. After a bag search we were given a guided tour of the stones: quartz, diamonds (ranging from small to large), on past the clasps and necklaces in precious stones to the crown of Peter the Great, his sceptre and orb, and jewellery belonging to his wife. We ended with lumps of gold and platinum.

I had an aching back, and saw Sergey at the book counter. Without being asked he had bought for us a CD of the Cathedral of the Archangel, cards, a book of photos in Russian and a smaller one in English, and a new guidebook, *Moscow Kremlin Red Square*. I was touched by his thoughtfulness.

Sergey a healer

We left the Kremlin and walked to the Moscow Cathedral (The Cathedral of Christ the Saviour) by the river. It was white with golden domes. It had been built in 1830, pulled down by Stalin and rebuilt after 1991. Easter was being observed that evening. It was the Russian Easter the next day. Putin would normally be there but he was returning from China. It was closed, so we walked to a nearby café, which was up steps, and I sat on a sofa with a cushion in my painful back and ordered a bottle of cold sparkling water, green tea and vanilla and chocolate ice-cream.

There was talk of my back. I described how I had slipped a disc in 1976 and had an ache in my lower back after a lot of walking. Sergey asked in Russian, "Is it number 3?" I stood up and invited him to touch, and he put his finger on the spot. He said in Russian that his fingers trembled, he knew it was number 3. I now realised he was a healer, like Rasputin, and felt instinctively where my pain was.

He offered to bring his "folding bed" to my room at 10.15am the next day, set it up and give me an hour's massage to get rid of my problem "300 per cent". I accepted but said it may be due to old age, the discs getting worn, the gelatine between them drying up, and if he couldn't help, thanks for trying. I joked he would be my Russian doctor.

I said to Igor as we left, "So we have General Igor and Colonel Igor and Dr Sergey." Sergey laughed a lot at this. I said, "English doctors arrange X-rays and recommend operations, Russian doctors do what the Romans did and what doctors were still doing until the First World War, push the disc back into place with force." He laughed and put his thumbs up.

Sergey was now my bodyguard. He stood above me while I sat on a seat in the metro and would not accept a free seat one down from me. He carried the bag of books and guarded me from possible attackers from both sides. After a stop we stood and shook hands with him and left him to go to his destination while we changed to go to Partizanskaya, the station for our hotel.

Igor said, "I've only spoken to him a couple of times until today." Earlier Sergey said he was in construction and imported coffee from Yemen. Hence Svetlana knew that the Triple Code began in Yemen and that the sva was there; and hence her certainty that the phoenix was in Yemen after it originated in Georgia.

Igor walked back to the hotel with us. He believed in Asian healing: acupuncture and gymnastics for the muscles surrounding veins (alternating between steam at 120C for 3 minutes and cold bath at 7C for 30 seconds to make the muscles move and pump blood). He was at ease with Sergey's approach to my back.

Igor and Engels

Igor said to me, "I am an atheist, everything is matter, Marx and Engels both said this." He had written a book, *The Dialectics of Matter*, in 1982 (published in 1997), modelled on Engels. I saw him as a dialectical materialist who had been misled by Marx and Engels into being non-spiritual, and ignoring the Light and the One that unites the universe. He had said to me, "You sound as if you're a Communist, like me," and I saw him as a loyal Communist (or Communist loyalist) who had stuck firm to the ideas of Engels who co-wrote much with Marx.

And he had benefited from the Communist system: he told me he had got the house he wanted as his mother had been married to a war hero and as she was a war widow he had some priority under the Chernenko Communist government, even though he was born in 1945 after his mother remarried.

At Igor's dacha

The next day, Sunday 28 April 2019, I woke with a painful right hand and wrist. It looked and felt broken and had bled and seemed inflamed. It was the Russian Easter Sunday, and there were coloured boiled eggs in the breakfast room.

Sergey brought a samovar Svetlana was giving us, and then sat in the lobby with us, waiting for Igor, who had said we were all going to his *dacha* and Sergey would do my massage there.

In the car, Svetlana said the only picture the main television news had shown of the event at the Moscow City Duma was of me shaking hands with Alexey Shaposhnikov, the Chairman of the Duma. Nothing else was shown.

The *dacha* was 30 kms outside Moscow. We passed through a forest of silver birch and entered a gated turning with individual *dacha*s on either side of a narrow road. I understood that Igor had had his *dacha* since 2001.

Slava was barbecuing at the back. We all sat in the grassy garden near a greenhouse and summerhouse and silver birches: Igor and Slava, Natasha's son Sacha and his girlfriend, Svetlana and Sergey, who was in a track suit. Then Sergey said he was ready for me.

We went into the *dacha*. He had set up his leather table in one of the rooms, and for half an hour I lay on my front with my face in the table's hole and he pressed my *chakra*s and checked that everything was normal and there were no spasms. We had a break, and I returned to have a full head-to-toe massage. His vigorous rubbing cured my back, but not my hand and wrist, despite the pressure he applied to them. I half-wondered if I had had a stroke and lost the use of my writing hand. I reckoned it was inflamed and took Nurofen, which Ann supplied.

Around 2.30pm we had lunch: barbecued chicken, onions and tomatoes, white bread and later a sausage each, with red wine, which my 'doctor' pronounced (Igor translated) as "obligatory, especially after a massage" (although he stuck to water). Svetlana had brought us nearly a dozen small presents: coffee from Yemen with curative properties, an owl for wisdom, a cornelian stone, rose quartz and three hearts, 30 stones for Ann, an egg, a doll whose clothes she had sewn, an angel she made for a month, and coloured eggs which we cracked over lunch and peeled their coloured paper and shells. Later their samovar made tea.

It was a traditional Russian Easter. Over the red wine there were speeches all round. They thanked us for coming, and we thanked them for what they had done. Ann called for international friendship. I toasted the younger generation. Slava and Sacha kindly said how "nice" we were. There were photos.

After lunch there was a tour of the house, all four floors. I spent some time in Igor's study. He showed me his book *The Dialectics of Matter*, and repeated, "I am an atheist, everything is matter, as Engels said." The rooms were refreshingly untidy and stacked with storage. There was a games room on the top floor and a billiard table, and a work room in the bottom-floor garage along with skis and snow boots for the winter. There was a netball net on the side of the house.

We then walked down to the river where he and Lidia were accustomed to swim in water with a temperature of 10C. He said his house had a 120C sauna, and he went out into the snow, but there was also a cold bath. And his South-Korean Bluepin-7 machine made his blood flow by squeezing his muscles.

We had tea and two cakes with icing and floral decorations. The samovar boiled water. There was blackcurrant tea in a teapot. A little was poured into a cup and topped up from the samovar. It was very 19th-century. The samovar Svetlana gave me came from Tula, 15 kms from Tolstoy's estate.

In Putin's rest-house: Barvikha sanatorium

Putin's rest-house-cum-sanatorium near Barvikha, seen from the entrance.

It was now time for me to change into a suit I had brought, and Igor and Svetlana drove us to Barvikha, which is on the south bank of the Moscow River surrounded by a pine forest, and Barvikha sanatorium, which has treated several Russian leaders including Boris Yeltsin and is run by the presidential administration's property department. It was opened in 1935 under Stalin, and has been the President's rest-house ever since. All the Soviet leaders after Stalin and the leaders of the Russian Federation have been there, and Churchill visited it. It was now Putin's rest-house.

It was huge: three large houses knocked together to give dozens of rooms for doctors. We were given a tour. The place was empty because it was Easter Sunday, and I saw a corridor with dozens of doors, each one for a specialist in a different disease so Putin, and government officials, could see the specialist they needed.

Eventually we were taken into a long room, and Ann and I were shown to a settee at the front of chairs on two sides of the room. Apart from Igor and Svetlana, there were three others in the room, including a man who supervised recordings.

In came Elena and Julia, who were sisters and Svetlana's cousins, and were performing a concert for me – in Putin's rest-house. There was an hour of Russian songs, with them looking at me and catching my eye when they could. I foot-tapped and smiled to show I was enjoying their concert.

Two ladies, Elena and Julia, in traditional Russian costume,
singing and dancing in a personal concert for Nicholas Hagger
in Putin's rest-house/sanatorium.

Then Igor stepped forward and made a speech and presented the two ladies with certificates certifying that they were members of the Universal State of the Earth. I was asked to make a short speech, after which I chatted with the two ladies. Julia had sung – or rather imitated – "bird song" from her throat very realistically, and said she had had the ability to sing from her throat since she was a child.

At school I sang Borodin's *Prince Igor* in the choir: "Sing we praises to our glorious Khan.... May our dancing give him pleasure, Khan Konchak, Khan Konchak." The two cousins had sung to me as if I was the Khan and had danced to give me pleasure. It was strange that Ann and I were the only real audience, that all the others had taken part in organising the event.

Svetlana had stayed at home the previous day to make phone calls relating to Putin, who was returning from China that day, and somehow she had been given permission to put on a special concert for me. It felt as if Putin, having been in Vladivostok meeting Kim Jong-un of North Korea and then in China all week, was considerately saying he was sorry he could not invite me to meet him in the Kremlin, but here was exclusive use of his rest-house and a concert to entertain me and thank me for visiting Russia – even though it was Svetlana and her cousins who had organised the entertainment.

We arrived back at the hotel around 10.30pm. We were told to expect a message at 10.30am next morning. If Svetlana and Igor had been able to get hold of the politician in the State Duma we would go to him. I should be prepared to hand over the letters and books for Putin and Elena Gagarina.

Waiting for calls from advisers to Putin that never came
The next day, our last full day in Moscow, Monday 29 April 2019, Easter Monday, I received Sergey at 10.30am and had a very firm, deep two-hour massage. Afterwards my back was substantially better, and the use of my right hand came back. I had full blood flow everywhere. There was no message from the Duma.

We were taken to an Uzbeki restaurant at 2.30pm for a farewell lunch, waiting for calls from two assistants to Putin, which never came, perhaps because it was Putin's first day back from China and there was no time, perhaps because it was the Russian Easter Monday and it was a holiday, a non-work day.

Svetlana told us she came from Uzbekistan in Central Asia in 1978, and Sergey came from Siberia in 1977. Both had previous families that ended in 1991 (the year the Soviet Union broke up and Communism ended). Rasputin had come from deep into Siberia (the village of Pokrovskoye) and as a healer had stopped the bleeding of the Tsar Nicholas II's haemophiliac son Alexei in 1908. Sergey was aware of being in the Rasputin tradition. He said he specialised in leeches, which suck out bad cholesterol.

We had pumpkin soup, pizza-looking triangles with different ingredients, thick slices of bread with poppy and cinnamon seeds, lumps of beef, rice, skewered meats and later chocolate-and-mango ice-cream. This took until 5.30pm.

I had taken books with me, and I now signed books for three assistants to Putin, which Svetlana undertook to deliver: Anatoly Karpov, President of the International Association of Peace Foundations and also the former world chess champion; Sergey Glazyev, a member of the Russian Academy of Sciences and adviser to Putin on regional economic integration from 2012 to 2019, who had *World Peace* and *World Constitution*; and Sergey Minonov, leader of the 'A Just Russia' political party, who had *World State*. I handed over the books I had signed to President Putin and the letter I had written him and the book and letter to Elena Gagarina.

We returned to the hotel to pack. My wrist swelled up again, and I took another anti-inflammatory tablet. For supper in the hotel (with Igor) we had lemon water, melon, papaya, meringue and yoghurt.

Sergey's Siberian shamanistic tradition
The next day, Tuesday 30 April, was our last day in Russia. Sergey arrived at 9.55am and massaged me for an hour and a half. At one point I briefly opened my eyes and saw him standing in trance, channelling energy from the air, and knew he was channelling power from the cosmos.

Igor was waiting in the lobby with Ann and Svetlana when we came down. We sat and talked. Svetlana said, "Sergey has not washed his hands for three days because they've touched Hagger," and everyone smiled. She said the present I was to have given to the Queen on her behalf in 2016 was the golden phoenix I was awarded. She said she would make another golden phoenix for Prince Charles.

We were taken to a final lunch at the 'Chocolate Café': mushroom soup, chicken salad, chicken cutlets, éclairs, vanilla-and-chocolate ice-cream, and blackcurrants in iced soda water (*kvass*, "Russian Pepsi").

I established that Sergey was from the Siberian shamanistic tradition, as was Rasputin. I said that in 10,000BC there were no doctors so you went to a shaman who was often in a cave. Sergey said in Russian, "I'd better start looking for a cave." He added, "I will be Rasputin to Nicholas's Tsar." He added that if my hand hurt on the flight I should put the cornelian stone Svetlana had given me on it and think of him, and he would cure it remotely.

Svetlana said, "You must return and meet the three assistants to Putin you signed books to, and Gorbachev, Elena Gagarina, and President Putin."

We set off for the airport later and there was an enormous traffic jam halfway there, and we were late. Slava took us as far as he was allowed to go. It took a long time to process our passports. The officer, in shirt and tie, put my opened passport face-down on his machine and kept looking at the screen, and I could see there were complications probably dating from the time our passports were confiscated at Vnukovo airport. We got through to the Space Lounge, which had a picture of Yuri Gagarin in a cosmonaut's helmet inside the door.

I had drafted most of a report on my time in Russia from 8.30 to midnight the previous evening, and I finished it now. I would send it to Eleanor Laing with a request that she would send it to Sir Alan Duncan in the Foreign Office, and he would reply that he was glad I had had a successful trip. I would also send it to Prince Charles's office, and would receive further best wishes from there.

The last I would hear from Svetlana was when on 22 March 2020 she asked me to invite Prince Charles to be the Chairman of the Board of Trustees of the World Ecological Foundation to work on creating eco-cities.

Her Financial Director Andrei Orlov sent me a letter to Prince

Charles dated 20 March signed by her, and under her signature was: WEF President, Baroness Svetlana Chumakova-Izmailovskaya. My signature was under hers with Chairman of WEF Board of Directors under my name. Andrei Orlov's signature was under mine with Financial Director of WEF Board of Directors under his name. At the very bottom of the letter was: Universal State of Earth (USE).

Svetlana told me on 25 March that an investor in the Netherlands had offered $1.3 billion as an initial amount. I wondered who would have access to this bank account.

I pointed out that the timing was bad as Prince Charles had just withdrawn to Scotland with Covid, and that there should be a website expressing the aim of the Trustees regarding eco-cities. I have not heard from her since.

I would later learn that Prince Charles was seeking permission to build an eco-city on 320 acres of wheat fields (and a cricket ground) he bought in south-east Faversham, Kent, in 1999 to become a second Poundbury with 2,500 eco-homes. I would also later learn that Prince Charles's eco-village on land bought with Dumfries House in 2007, Knockroon, had got into difficulties since the first houses were bought in 2012, and Lord Brownlow had bailed it out with £1.7 million. A possible Russian solution had been offered in the committee Svetlana wanted Prince Charles to chair.

After we boarded our plane and sat in the same seats as when we arrived, in 8A and 8C next to each other in the Club area, words Svetlana spoke in Natasha's apartment (see p.35) rang in my ears: "If you are writing a book about your visit to Russia, it should be called *The Golden Phoenix*." And, full of warmth at the reception I had had, the awards I had been given and the kindness of our hosts and so many of the Russians I had encountered, I knew that when the time came that would be my title; and that if, having been sung to in his rest-house-cum-sanatorium, I was invited back to meet Putin and become his world-peace adviser, then I would return.

That was two years ten months before Russia's invasion of Ukraine turned Putin into our Hitler; made the Russian approaches to me in retrospect appear manipulative; and cast a nationalistic shadow across my inaugurating a new age and world empire and my calls for a democratic, partly-federal World State's universal peace two miles from the Kremlin on 22 April 2019.

It made me wonder whether I had been approached to bring in an undemocratic Russian Universal State of the Earth and Supreme Council of Humanity in 2015, to be based in the Globe Center; whether the General wanted me to front a book advocating closed space and denying the existence of all nuclear weapons except for North Korea's to discredit my democratic, partly-federal World State; and whether on 22 April 2019 I had inaugurated a new Russian age and world empire, a Russian Universal State, before the Admiral and Vice-Admiral held my hands aloft on stage.

A new Russian world order would get back Russia's pre-1991 territories and rule from Lisbon to Vladivostok, the "common economic space" Putin had foreseen in 2010, now Russian. I was glad I had called for a democratic World State and world peace in my speech in Moscow but it now seemed that I was up against insurmountable nationalism. It felt as if I had been calling for world peace two miles from Hitler's Chancellery in 1938.

2

Ukraine:
Why Russia's Invasion of Ukraine Happened,
and a New Russian World Order

The Russian invasion of Ukraine from March 2021 to 24 February 2022

The Russian plan to invade Ukraine seems to have developed early. The Russian military build-up began on the Russian-Ukrainian border in March and April 2021. There was another build-up in both Russia and Belarus from October 2021 to February 2022, apparently conducting exercises. These timings are important as they suggest that the invasion of Ukraine was already being considered in Moscow before March 2021. It was a long-term plan, not a sudden decision.

The Russian demands on 17 December 2021 were that the US and NATO should enter into a legally-binding agreement to stop Ukraine from ever joining NATO, and to remove NATO's multi-national forces from its member states in Eastern Europe. By the end of 2021 there were believed to be 190,000 troops and equipment on the Russian side of its border with Ukraine.

There were clashes in Donbas from 17 to 21 February 2022, and both pro-Russian Ukrainians and pro-Ukrainian Ukrainians in Donbas accused each other of firing across the borders of their territories. On 21 February 2022 Putin sent Russian troops into Donbas as a "peace-keeping mission", allegedly to cope with these "illegal" border infringements. On 24 February Putin announced a "special military operation" in eastern Ukraine, which was effectively a declaration of war.

We need to consider why and at what stage Putin decided to invade Ukraine, and we have just seen that the decision seems to have been taken before March 2021. Before we can dwell on the reasons for the invasion, we need to consider an overview of the events in Ukraine from February 2022 until August 2022.

The invasion did not go according to Russia's plan

The invasion of Ukraine itself did not go according to Russia's plan.

The first phase of the invasion was from Belarus and targeted Kyiv. There were also invasions from Crimea in the south and from south-east Russia to target Luhansk and Donetsk. The attack on Kyiv captured surrounding towns by 5 March but failed because a convoy of tanks 40 miles long stalled with supply-chain problems, and an airborne assault failed to capture a key airport. Volodymyr Zelensky, the President of Ukraine, was supposed to have been killed and Kyiv was supposed to fall and the whole of Ukraine become Russian by 8 March. The Russians withdrew and regrouped to take the eastern part of Ukraine.

The second phase of the invasion involved a south-eastern offensive on Donbas, Mykolaiv and Odesa, Dnipro and Zaporizhzhia (where Europe's largest nuclear power station has been occupied and used as a base from which to launch missiles), and Mariupol, which eventually fell on 18 May 2022. There was a naval conflict on the Black Sea, and the Russian flagship *Moskva* (which features at the back of Admiral Popovich's book) was sunk on 14 April 2022 after being hit by two Ukrainian anti-ship missiles, with allegedly up to 250 killed (according to Ukrainian sources).

Six months after the invasion, on 24 August 2022, Russia was in possession of two-thirds of the Donbas region including Kherson and Lysychansk, and was digging in for the winter, its offensive having stalled. It was estimated to have had 45,400 Russian troops killed. Ukraine was trying to take back Kherson before the winter and had attacked a Russian airbase in Crimea, detonating aviation ammunition with long-range heavy missiles supplied by the US, fired 180 miles away.

Throughout the end of February, March, April and May 2022 residential buildings in central, southern and eastern parts of Ukraine were shelled indiscriminately, and the suffering of individuals was appalling. There were obvious war crimes: violations of the laws of war, especially the intentional killing of civilians. The 6.7 million refugees (according to the UN) mostly headed to the West via Poland, mainly women and children as the men were required to stay and fight in the popular resistance.

On 24 May 2022 Ukraine's head of the Ministry of Defence's Main Directorate of Intelligence, Kyrylo Budanov, said that President Putin could have several more years to live despite suffering from serious illnesses, including Parkinson's disease and recently having an operation for cancer. He also said that there had been an assassination attempt on Putin in March 2022. On 10 June 2022 a Kremlin insider reported that Putin was given "urgent medical help" after falling ill while talking to military chiefs, and doctors advised him not to make any lengthy public appearances. In July 2022 Putin was reported as swatting away mosquitoes near the right side of his face with his left hand while his right arm hung limp, and also as walking with a slight limp.

There was general alarm that Russia might use its tactical nuclear weapons. Some Russian statements confirmed that it would, others denied it, but Russia was reported to be continuing to test its hypersonic long-range international ballistic missile RS-28 Sarmat, known as Satan 2, which has a speed of 25,500 kms per hour (15,844 mph) and would only take two-and-a-half minutes to destroy the UK or France. It was reported that in the autumn of 2022 Russia would be supplying its navy (including its Black Sea fleet) with Zircon hypersonic missiles which can travel at nine times the speed of sound.

Foreign allies of Ukraine sent military aid. On 26 February the US authorised 350 million dollars' worth of military assistance – anti-armour and anti-aircraft systems – and the next day the EU said it would purchase and send to Ukraine 450 million euros' worth of lethal assistance and an additional 50 million euros' worth of non-lethal supplies. The UK also supplied Ukraine with Javelin anti-tank weapons. There was general unease at the prospect of an escalation of the conflict into the Third World War.

It was impossible to determine the precise number of casualties, and both sides gave low estimates of their own forces killed and high estimates of their opponents' forces killed. In mid-July 2022, Admiral Sir Tony Radakin, Head of the British Armed Forces, reckoned 50,000 Russians had been killed or injured, 1,700 Russian tanks and nearly 4,000 armoured vehicles had been destroyed during the 150 days since the beginning of the Russian invasion, and Russia only had 10 per cent of Ukraine and was struggling to occupy 20 per cent. According to new classified UK intelligence more than 75,000 Russian soldiers had been killed or injured in Ukraine, a loss equivalent to almost the entire British army and half the 150,000 Russian troops who took part in the invasion of Ukraine. By 24 August 2022, six months after the Russian invasion, a third of Ukraine's population had been displaced, but Ukraine had retaken an area in the north the size of Denmark that had previously been captured by Russia.

Ukraine's counter-offensive, Russia's annexation of four regions, the US's apparent cutting of four pipelines and Russia's Poseidon nuclear weapons

In late August 2022, a pre-winter Ukrainian counter-offensive retook 3,000 (Ukraine claimed 6,000) square kilometres in the north-east, including Izium and Kharkov. The largest natural-gas reserves in eastern Ukraine, which include the large deposit discovered in 2012 (see p.75), are in the Kharkov and Poltava regions, and one of the aims of the counter-offensive was to take back control and defend these natural-gas reserves from Russian occupation and exploitation. This counter-offensive opened up a third phase in the war, after Russia's invasion and the battle of Donbas. Kherson was threatened with being surrounded. Following a visit to Samarkand to meet the leaders of China, India and Turkey, who harangued him, Putin announced a partial mobilisation of 300,000 reservists (seemingly in addition to the 130,000 conscripts drafted in the spring and now trained and ready to serve), and there were rumours that actually 1 million Russian troops would be sent in an effort to stave off defeat. Russia began bombing Ukrainian dams to flood military crossing points in order to halt the counter-offensive.

At the same time he announced the partial mobilisation Putin warned that he might use nuclear weapons if Russia was threatened, and that he was "not bluffing". Russia then held a referendum, and in the Kremlin on 30 September 2022 declared the annexed parts of north-eastern Ukraine Russian: the Luhansk, Donetsk (without Lyman, which Ukraine soon recaptured), Zaporizhzhia and Kherson regions comprising 15 per cent of Ukraine's territory, the biggest annexation since the Second World War. Zelensky responded by asking NATO to fast-track Ukraine's accession to the bloc. The annexation meant that an attack on the Russian-held parts of the four annexed regions should be regarded as an attack on Russia and could therefore be resisted with tactical nuclear weapons. Jake Sullivan, the US national security adviser, said that the US had "communicated directly and privately to the Russians at a very high level" how it would respond with "catastrophic" action if Putin carried out his nuclear-strike threat. Many believed that Ukraine and the West were one step nearer to a nuclear attack.

Meanwhile, from 25 to 28 September 2022 (shortly before the annexation and in retaliation for the four referendums which ran from 23 to 27 September) four Nord Stream 1 and 2 pipelines were sabotaged at a depth of 80 metres (260 feet) so natural gas bubbled up to the surface of the Baltic Sea in international waters off Denmark, filling the atmosphere with methane. Deep-sea divers from a Norwegian mine-hunter attached C-4 plastic explosives with timing devices to the four pipelines. A plane then dropped a sonar buoy whose low-frequency sounds set off the timing devices at different times and created four massive leaks. It seemed that these four pipelines would not be operational again, shutting down a project estimated to be worth £35 billion. It was unlikely that Europeans would buy Russian natural gas in future. Four referendums and, a day or two after, each of the four pipelines – surely not a coincidence.

At first it was thought that Putin was responsible for the sabotage, but why would Russia sabotage its own natural-gas supply to Germany that was paying for the Russia-Ukraine war? Then a former Polish minister, Radoslaw Sikorski, posted a picture of one of the leaks and a comment, "Thank you, USA", and raised the possibility that the US was responsible (see pp.86–87 for further evidence that the US wished to end Germany's reliance on Russian natural gas). If so, the attack on the four pipelines was a US/NATO act of war against Russia and made the widening and escalation of the war more likely. The Russia-Ukraine war had now reached the Baltic Sea.

Putin was well-known for believing that all the world's troubles were caused by Western aggression (in Vietnam, Iraq, Afghanistan and elsewhere), and it was known that he wanted to punish the UK for supporting Ukraine. There was speculation regarding Putin's retaliation against the US and UK. Putin's AS-31 *Losharik* spy submarines could be conveyed from the Arctic to the Atlantic beneath a 'mothership', the 604-foot, 30,000-ton K-329 *Belgorod* submarine, the world's biggest submarine potentially armed with eight Poseidon nuclear torpedoes each 79 feet long, a new type of weapon, a doomsday device that can trigger a 1,600-foot nuclear tsunami which drowns and irradiates coastal cities. It was believed to be in the Arctic waters in early October 2022.

The *Belgorod* might attack the undersea data cables that carry the internet and financial information (involving $9.2 trillion of daily financial transactions with the UK) from the US across the Atlantic to the UK, which was vulnerable to a submarine attack on these cables. If they were breached the UK's internet would be shut down, there would be a disastrous impact on stock markets, and communications with the overseas military would be damaged. The North Sea might also be targeted, not just the Atlantic: pipelines (including two supplying the UK with oil and gas from Norway), rigs and undersea cables, damage to which would cause a massive recession in the UK and deprive the UK population of heat during the coming winter. The pipelines, rigs and cables that were vital to the UK's quality of life were now at risk, and the UK sent a type-23 frigate and a survey ship to guard the gas pipes from Norway by scanning the seabed for signs of interference such as mines and monitors on cables and pipes.

The Chechen leader Ramzan Kadyrov, an ally of Putin, called for Putin to unleash tactical low-yield nuclear weapons on Ukraine. On 3 October 2022 a nuclear military train operated by Moscow's nuclear division was spotted and videoed at Sergiyev Posad north-east of Moscow, possibly heading for Ukraine. It was hauling upgraded armoured personnel carriers said to contain equipment for nuclear weapons. An ex-British Army intelligence officer said that the train had "all the signatures of the 12th Main Directorate", which is responsible for transporting Russia's nuclear arsenal. The signature equipment was "a BPM-97 armoured vehicle", which has been used by the 12th Main Directorate. NATO had warned the leaders of its member nations that there would be a test of Poseidon, a nuclear-capable torpedo drone known as the "weapon of the apocalypse", in the Black Sea as "a signal to the West". The train was carrying the means of making such a test possible. Russia seemed to be preparing its population for nuclear warfare by showing atomic explosions on its propaganda TV channels with the title: "In anticipation of nuclear conflict – how weapons of mass destruction have become part of the geopolitical game."

In mid-November 2022 Russia's defence minister evacuated most of the Russian army's troops from Kherson, fearing encirclement. They withdrew across the River Dnipro to defend its territory on the eastern bank of the river during the coming winter. The withdrawal, described by Russia as a strategic movement of troops and by Ukraine as a rout, was humiliating for Russia, coming only weeks after Putin announced that Kherson would be Russian for ever, and put pressure on Putin who may have been looking for peace in a negotiated form (see pp.**154–155**).

Everyone was wary. Russian troops had destroyed all the infrastructure and had left Kherson without power, water and food, threatening a humanitarian catastrophe, and there was a fear that some troops had stayed behind in civilian clothes to launch a guerrilla war of street-fighting, or that a tactical nuclear weapon would now flatten Kherson. In mid-November Russia launched a barrage of missiles across Ukraine targeting electricity and heating infrastructure, and plunged much of Ukraine into darkness.

There was general agreement that in the first three months of the war Russia had 15,000 troops killed, the same number of the Soviet Union's dead in nine years of fighting in Afghanistan. There were estimates in November 2022 that both Russia and Ukraine had had 100,000 killed.

In early 2023 Russia seemed to be making progress. In mid-January 2023 Russian Wagner mercenaries captured Soledar and threatened to cut off Ukrainian forces in the next town Bakhmut, with 500,000 Russian troops reported to be heading to Ukraine for a spring offensive. However, according to US intelligence (revealed at a Western summit at Ramstein Air Base in southern Germany on

20 January 2023) Russian casualties in Ukraine had reached 188,000 with 2,000 tanks destroyed or captured (compared with 15,000 troops killed and 35,000 wounded in the Soviet occupation of Afghanistan from 1979 to 1989).

The background: 'Rockefellers', Stalin, oil and natural gas

We have now seen the stage the Russian invasion of Ukraine had reached by August 2022, and we can now consider how and why Putin took his decision to invade. Although the decision seems to have been reached in principle before March 2021, few predicted there would be an invasion of Ukraine. Some believed that Putin was bluffing. To understand the reasons Putin gave for the Russian invasion of Ukraine which began on 24 February 2022 we must look at the background to the conflict in 1925–1926, and from 1996, which involves 'Rockefellers' of the Syndicate', oil and natural gas.

In *The Fall of the West* I described how 'Rockefellers' were behind Stalin and from 1926 financed his five-year plans (the first one through Schiff's Kuhn, Loeb and Co., who now acted for 'Rockefellers'),[1] in return for a half-interest in Russian oil, including Baku's oil in Azerbaijan, which they bought in 1925.[2] 'Rockefellers' then planned oil pipelines from Baku to the vicinity of the Black Sea.[3]

Gazprom

'Rockefellers' had talks with Gorbachev. They were now deeply involved in piping Russian oil. After Gorbachev left office in December 1991 the Gorbachev Foundation (whose building I visited, see pp.38–39) was capitalised in the US with $3 million from the Carnegie Endowment for International Peace, the Ford Foundation, the Pew and Melon Funds – and the Rockefeller Brothers Fund.[4] The support of the Rockefeller brothers for Gorbachev suggests that 'Rockefellers' supported Gorbachev's *perestroika* (restructuring) and *glasnost* (openness), and that these may have been a 'Rockefellerite' ploy to bring about new 'Rockefellerite' pipelines.

Gazprom, which deals in oil and gas, was founded in August 1989 with headquarters in St Petersburg. The Soviet Union became a major producer of natural gas following discoveries of large natural-gas reserves in Siberia and the Ural and Volga regions under the Ministry of Gas Industry (created in 1965). In August 1989 under the leadership of Viktor Chernomyrdin (the Minister of Gas Industry), the Ministry of Gas Industry transformed itself into State Gas Concern (shortened in Russian to 'Gazprom'). The company was still controlled by the State but the control was exercised through shares of stock, with the State owning 100 per cent.

After the collapse of the Soviet Union in 1991, Boris Yeltsin made Chernomyrdin his Prime Minister in December 1992, and Gazprom was privatised. It became a joint-stock company in 1993. In 1994 33 per cent of Gazprom's shares were owned by individuals, 15 per cent as stock by employees and the State retained 40 per cent (later lowered to 38 per cent).

Chernomyrdin was able to ensure that the State did not regulate Gazprom, which was able to evade taxes and avoid paying the State large dividends. Board members and management launched massive asset-stripping and Gazprom's property passed to them and their relatives and favoured friends.

In 1996 Chernomyrdin was in partnership with David Rockefeller, and he sold the energy assets of the new Commonwealth of Independent States (CIS) to 'Rockefellers' for knock-down prices.[5] Much of Gazprom was sold via banks that seem to have acted as fronts for 'Rockefellers' for $294 million, though valued at $3.4 billion; and United Energy Systems, the Soviet Union's power and utility generator, was sold to 'Rockefellers' for $467 million, though valued at $3 billion.[6]

Yeltsin fired Chernomyrdin as Prime Minister in 1998, and he returned to Gazprom as the Chairman of the Board of Directors. Soon after he came to power in 2000, Putin fired Chernomyrdin from his position on Gazprom, and Putin also sorted out Rem Vyakhirev, the co-founder of Gazprom. They were replaced by Dmitry Medvedev (Chairman) and Alexi Miller (CEO), who were to stop the asset-stripping. The gas producer Itera was forced to sell stolen assets back to Gazprom.

In 2005 a State-owned company, Rosneftegaz, bought a 10.7399-per-cent share of Gazprom, and this, together with its 40-per-cent share of the State Property Committee, gave the Russian government ownership of 50 per cent, and control, of Gazprom. In 2007 Gazprom and the Italian company Eni SpA agreed to construct a natural-gas pipeline from Russia to Europe: the South Stream pipeline that would run under the Black Sea to Bulgaria with a south fork to Italy and a north fork to Hungary. This was cancelled by the Russian government in 2014.[7]

By participating in the breaking-up of the USSR into independent republics via Gorbachev, and then by participating in the asset-stripping of 1996, 'Rockefellers', who had already owned a half-share in Soviet oil since 1925, were able to pipe oil and natural gas under the Caspian Sea to the west, south and east. Geologists have estimated there is $200 billion worth of oil under the Caspian Sea.[8]

'Rockefellers' had long planned oil pipelines from Baku to the vicinity of the Black Sea: Baku–Georgia–Supsa on the Black Sea, and Baku–Georgia–Ceyhan in Turkey.[9] Both pipelines are controlled by the British-led Azerbaijan International Oil Co. (AIOC), which is headed by the BP Group (created by British Petroleum merged with AMOCO, formerly the 'Rockefellerite' Standard Oil of Indiana).[10]

The Russians had alternative pipelines: Baku–Chechnya–Novorossiysk on the Black Sea and Tengiz (Kazakhstan)–Novorossiysk.

Russia's natural gas through Ukraine
There is a long history of Russia bringing natural gas from the Black Sea to Europe.

The Russian Trans-Ukrainian natural-gas pipeline from Russia through Ukraine (Urengoy–Pomary–Uzhgorod in Ukraine), also known as the Trans-Siberian pipeline, was completed in 1982–1984, and there were several subsequent pipelines from Russia to Europe through Ukraine, some from the Black Sea.[11] In 2012 Russia supplied 39 per cent of the EU's natural gas.

Of the three major Russian pipelines to the EU, two natural-gas pipelines ran from Russia through central Ukraine: Soyuz to the north, which branches with a north fork going to Austria and Germany, and a south fork through Romania to Turkey; and Brotherhood, which, like Soyuz, joins the Yamal–Europe pipeline and ends in Austria and Germany, with a south fork to northern Italy. (See map on p.75.)

In 2012 enormous gas reserves (2.3 trillion cubic metres) were discovered under Ukraine's share of the Black Sea. Russia tried to negotiate access to the new deposits, but talks collapsed. Another major deposit of natural gas was discovered in eastern Ukraine. In 2013 Ukraine reached an agreement with Royal Dutch Shell to start drilling in eastern Ukraine.

In April 2013 the Ukrainian Minister of Energy and Coal Industry announced that the projects in eastern Ukraine and under the Black Sea around Crimea would soon start producing so much natural gas that Ukraine would no longer need to import natural gas from Russia or anywhere else; and that Ukraine would become a net exporter of natural gas to Europe, and compete with Russia by 2020. This would end Putin's leverage over Europe.[12]

In 2014 Russia's Gazprom controlled a fifth of the world's gas

Map showing Soyuz and Brotherhood natural-gas pipelines passing through Russia and Ukraine (see pp.74, 76).

reserves and supplied more than half Ukraine's gas and 30 per cent of Europe's gas annually. Ukraine, long important because it is a corridor for Russia's Soyuz and Brotherhood natural-gas pipelines (see map on p.85), had now become a competitor that threatened Russia's oil and gas exports.[13]

The US now intervened in Ukrainian politics. In December 2013 US Assistant Secretary of State Victoria Nuland confirmed the US had invested over $5 billion to ensure "a secure and prosperous and democratic Ukraine". In January 2014 the US energy giant Chevron signed a $10-billion shale gas deal with Ukraine that "the ex-Soviet nation hopes could end its energy dependence by 2020". The deal would allow Chevron to explore the Olesky deposit in western Ukraine that Kyiv estimated can hold 2.98 trillion cubic metres of gas, and similar deals were reached with Shell and ExxonMobil.

A conversation between Nuland and the US Ambassador to Kyiv, Geoffrey Pyatt, leaked on 7 February 2014, showed that the US was liaising with opposition parties to manipulate the Ukrainian government into acting in accordance with US interests. Russia accused US gas companies Chevron and Exxon of encroaching on Gazprom's regional monopoly in Ukraine. As we have seen Ukraine was a crucial connection for Russian gas to Europe (Germany) and Asia (Kazakhstan), and it was then holding 395 million barrels of oil reserves.

Conflict between Russia and Ukrainian Crimea

In *The Fall of the West* I described the removal of Ukraine's pro-Russian President and Russia's annexation of Crimea to cope with this situation:[14]

> A conflict between Russia and the Ukraine began in February 2014, centring on the Ukrainian regions of Crimea and Donbas. The Russians removed [i.e. gave sanctuary to] the Ukrainian President Viktor Yanukovych on 22 February 2014, and Russian soldiers without insignias took control of the Crimea, which had always given Russia access to the Black Sea. After a Russian-organised referendum Crimea was annexed in March. In April pro-Russian separatists in Donbas declared two People's Republics. With the

support of the Russian military Ukrainian forces were defeated in December. The ensuing war was still continuing in 2021.

In March 2014 the Republic of Crimea's Deputy Prime Minister Rustam Temirgaliev announced that Gazprom would take over the ownership of Ukraine's State-owned oil and gas company Naftogaz. On 1 April Russia's energy minister Alexander Novak said Gazprom would finance an undersea gas pipeline to Crimea. A trans-Black-Sea undersea pipeline from Anapa, near the Crimea, to Turkey, a joint venture including Gazprom, began in January 2020.

The Syndicate's pipelines were behind the Russian-Ukrainian war and the annexation of Crimea. The Syndicate was behind the invasion of Crimea as Sevastopol in the Crimea is central to the northern shore of the Black Sea and is very near Novorossiysk, the largest Russian port and the largest port in the Black Sea. The Crimea is a base that can protect the shipping and export of oil reaching Novorossiysk via the two Russian pipelines: the Russian Baku–Chechnya–Novorossiysk and the Russian Tengiz (Kazakhstan)–Novorossiysk pipelines. The Crimea also affords a Russian base from which to defend Russian pipelines that cross the Ukraine to Crimea and cross the Black Sea.

In 2019 Gazprom was the largest publicly listed natural gas company in the world and the largest company in Russia by revenue. In 2018 Gazprom's sales were 8.2 trillion roubles with a profit of 1.2 trillion roubles. In 2020 its sales were 6.3 trillion roubles, 8.1 per cent down because of Covid. In 2021 sales increased to 10.2 trillion roubles.

It is clear from the above that a key factor in the background to Russia's invasion of Ukraine is Russia's determination that Gazprom's natural-gas pipelines should continue through Ukraine, and that Ukraine is seeking to be a natural-gas competitor to Russia, with the aid of Royal Dutch Shell.

There is a Syndicate dimension to the competition between Gazprom and Royal Dutch Shell: 'Rockefellerite' Gazprom has profited from sending Russia's gas from the Black Sea across Ukraine to Europe, and 'Rothschildite' Royal Dutch Shell, who have been drilling in East Ukraine, have been helping Ukraine to end its dependence on

Russian/'Rockefellerite' energy. Both 'Rockefellers' and 'Rothschilds' are the key institutions in, and share power within, the Bilderberg Group. They are fierce in competition with each other, but share power at the annual Bilderberg-Group meetings and both advance the cause of the Syndicate and co-operate in shaping its future policy.

Russia's nationalistic history

While this was happening to natural gas, which sucked in US interest in Ukraine behind Chevron and Exxon, Russian nationalism was stirring over Ukraine. Ukraine had been part of Scythia in Roman times and was part of the medieval state of Kyivan Rus, which disintegrated in the 12th century. Modern Russia, Belarus and Ukraine all claim the peoples of Kyivan Rus as their cultural ancestors.

Ukraine was ruled by the external Mongolian Golden Horde, the Grand Duchy of Lithuania and the Kingdom of Poland, and the Crimean Khanate, and eventually passed to the Russian Empire and Habsburg Austria.

The Russian Revolution of 1917 brought warfare, and Ukrainian Bolsheviks established the Ukrainian Soviet Socialist Republic, which became one of the founding republics of the Soviet Union. Ukraine was part of the Soviet Union in Lenin's early days, and between 4 and 5 million Ukrainian peasants died of famine deliberately created by Stalin to control rebellious peasants in 1932–1933. Putin later denied this famine took place and declined to see it as a reason for Ukrainians to turn against Russia. Ukraine extended westwards after 1939 and was occupied by the Axis during the Second World War.

Ukrainians fought both Germany and the Soviet Union for independence, and in 1945 became one of the founding members of the UN. In 1953 the Ukrainian Nikita Khrushchev became head of the Communist Party of the Soviet Union, and Ukraine expanded southwards with Khrushchev's assistance. Crimea was transferred from Russia to Ukraine. Ukraine had therefore effectively been Russian for a long while, and after the collapse of the Soviet Union in 1991 it became independent.

Ukraine's presidential election in November 2004 between pro-European Viktor Yushchenko and pro-Russian Viktor Yanukovych was rigged to declare Yanukovych the winner. There were extensive protests, known as the Orange Revolution, and a revote in January 2005 declared Yushchenko the clear winner.

Putin's meteoric rise from being a KGB officer in Dresden and later Head of the FSB (Russia's Federal Security Service, a federal executive body for national security and the main successor agency to the KGB) ended in his becoming in 1999 one of three first deputy prime ministers to Yeltsin and on the same day Yeltsin's acting Prime Minister. He succeeded Yeltsin as President in 2000 and is thought to have been behind a ruthless FSB attack on Chechnya's Grozny that was blamed on Chechnyan rebels. Putin's ruthless warfare on Chechnya (which is between the Black Sea and Caspian Sea) began in 1999 as a "special military operation" and resulted in a puppet state there in 2009.

After an eight-year recession and a damaged economy following the 2008 financial crisis, under Yushchenko, Ukraine had an association agreement with the EU, which on 21 November 2013 his successor in 2010, the pro-Russian President Viktor Yanukovych, suspended. There were protests by pro-European Ukrainians in Kyiv's central square, Maidan Nezalezhnosti (Independence Square, Maidan for short). In February 2014 millions of Ukrainians took to the streets to protest at the severing of the association agreement with the EU, and "Euromaidan", the "Revolution of Dignity", took place. The Ukrainian Parliament impeached Yanukovych on 22 February 2014, the day Putin removed him to Russia.

There is some evidence that this impeachment was orchestrated by the US to achieve a regime change while the US pushed to expand NATO eastwards and to establish friendly relations with Ukraine. The election of Petro Poroshenko in May 2014 may also have been orchestrated by the US.[15] This 'coup' that brought in pro-NATO, anti-Russian leadership was overseen within the US by then Vice-President Joe Biden.

On 22–23 February 2014 Russian forces entered Crimea, which Russia controlled from 1783 under Catherine the Great, and was an ancestral territory Kyivan Rus' wrested from the Byzantines in 988, and the Russian-Ukrainian war began. There was unrest in the Russian-speaking east and south of Ukraine, which supported Yanukovych.

A referendum was held among the ethnic Russians of Crimea, and Russia then annexed Crimea on 18 March 2014. A war started in the Donbas region, in the Donetsk and Luhansk 'oblasts' (separatist statelets), between on one side pro-Ukrainian Ukrainians and on the other side pro-Russian Ukrainians and Russian mercenaries. This war has continued until 2022, and the State Duma of Russia "recognised" Donetsk and Luhansk on 21 February 2022, with annexations that have followed after referendums.

During his time as President, Putin made several statements in which he stood for Greater Russia and wanted the principalities that had been removed from the USSR in 1991, and had been given governments and parliaments, to be returned to Russia like Chechnya and Crimea. He believed that without Ukraine Russia could not be a superpower and several times said that he did not believe in Western democracy or that Ukraine is a proper independent country. Putin seemed to believe that to allow democratic expression in Ukraine was a threat as there would then be a popular demand for democratic expression in Russia.

Russia's historical aim in Ukraine

So besides ending Ukrainian-Royal Dutch Shell drilling for natural gas, Russia's invasion of Ukraine was also to put an end to the separatists from pro-Russian rule in the self-proclaimed Donetsk People's Republic and Luhansk People's Republic. These separatists were called "neo-Nazis" because the wartime separatists fought the Soviet Union for independence during the Second World War while trying to free Ukraine from both Axis and Soviet occupation, and were branded supporters of Nazi Germany.

Russia's strategic aim was to annex Donetsk and Luhansk, which has happened, and seize the southern part of Ukraine along the Black Sea from the Russian Donbas lands, to Moldova and join up with pro-Russian Transnistria. It was also to occupy central Ukraine, the territory through which the Soyuz and Brotherhood natural-gas pipelines pass, so the pipelines could be guarded securely and Ukraine could be blocked from competing with Russian natural gas by developing huge new deposits of natural gas in eastern and western

Ukraine and under the Black Sea.

In this strategic aim Putin was using his military to support Gazprom in sealing off Ukraine's natural gas while supporting old-style Russian imperialism.

Russia seems to have returned to the old nationalistic expansionist Tsars' Russian Empire. Its nationalism is the opposite of the supranationalism of my democratic World State which I had explained in Moscow, and Russia's invading of Ukraine seems to support my intuitive feeling that the military men in my audience in Moscow on 22 April 2019 were in their minds attending the inauguration of a *Russian* world empire.

Putin's speech on 24 February 2022

In a pre-dawn TV address on 24 February 2022 Putin declared that Russia could not feel "safe, develop and exist", because of an alleged constant threat from Ukraine. He spoke of "events taking place in the Donbas and the key issues of ensuring the security of Russia itself". He said "we see that the forces that carried out a *coup d'état* in Ukraine in 2014, seized power and are holding it with the help of... decorative electoral procedures have finally abandoned the peaceful settlement of the conflict. For eight years... we have done everything possible to resolve the situation by peaceful, political means."

He said:[16]

> "The People's Republics of Donbas turned to Russia with a request for help.
>
> "In this regard, in accordance with Article 51 of Part 7 of the UN Charter, with the approval of the Federation Council of Russia and in pursuance of the treaties of friendship and mutual assistance ratified by the Duma on 22 February with the Donetsk People's Republic and the Luhansk People's Republic, I decided to launch a special military operation.
>
> "Its goal is to protect people who have been subjected to abuse and genocide by the regime in Kyiv for eight years. And for this we will pursue the demilitarisation and denazification of Ukraine, as well as bringing to justice those who committed numerous bloody

crimes against civilians, including citizens of the Russian Federation.

"Our plans do not include the occupation of Ukrainian territories. We are not going to impose anything on anyone by force."

The "abuse and genocide" he alleged was the support the regime in Kyiv gave to the pro-Ukrainians in Donetsk and Luhansk, and it has been estimated that between 2014 and 2022 14,000 Ukrainian Russians were killed by the Ukrainian military and separatist battalions.[17] The "demilitarisation and denazification" he spoke of was the plan to expel the pro-Ukrainians in Donetsk and Luhansk so the Ukrainian killing in the two statelets he had recognised could stop and the two statelets could be ultimately annexed by Russia, as has happened, like Crimea.

He referred to a "special military operation", which at one level was to get rid of the pro-Ukrainians in Donetsk and Luhansk. But there might be a reference to another event.

According to *Tass*, on 22 January 2022 the Commander of the Ukrainian National Guard, Colonel-General Nikolai Balan, issued an order to assault the Donbas People's Republics of Donetsk and Luhansk by co-ordinating the battalion tactical group with the 80th Separate Airborne Assault Brigade of the Ukrainian Armed Forces. This brigade had been trained by US and British instructors in accordance with NATO training programs since 2016. The attack was to take place "in March 2022". The Russian Defence Ministry allegedly got hold of this plan.[18]

It may be that this secret document pushed Putin into intervening in Ukraine on 24 February 2022 before the Ukrainian offensive could take place, so Russian forces could either disarm or neutralise the Ukrainian military. The "special military operation" could have been triggered to block the threat of this alleged attack by Ukraine on Donetsk and Luhansk. The threat of this intervention could have been responsible for Russia's emphasis that NATO should never enter Ukraine and should withdraw its bases from the east to the pre-1997 geographical positions.[19]

However, we have seen that Russia's decision to invade Ukraine seems to have been taken before March 2021, when build-ups started happening, and the leaked plan could be misinformation, to justify an invasion planned over a year previously. The "special military operation" may not have been to block this intervention in Donbas, but simply to return Donetsk and Luhansk to Russian rule, and create a land bridge between Russia and Crimea to safeguard Russian access to the Black Sea and beyond.

It could also be that Putin, suspecting the US of being behind the impeachment of Yanukovych, also suspected the US of intending a regime change in Russia, and that Putin was willing to destroy Ukraine to prevent this.[20]

US involvement in Ukraine

The special operation could have been designed to block increasing American interest in Ukraine following the events of 2013–2014 and during the next eight years.

For the background we need to go back to 1989, and the proposal Gorbachev made to the US that the Soviet Union would withdraw from Eastern Europe and allow Germany to be reunited. (See Hannes Adomeit, 'Gorbachev's Consent to Unified Germany's Membership in NATO', paper delivered to the conference on 'Europe and the End of the Cold War at the Sorbonne Université, Paris on 15–17 June 2005, revised on 1 November 2006, 20 pages, swp-Berlin.org/publications/products/arbeitspapiere/Consent_to_Nato_ks.pdf.)

Russians have since stated that this was on the condition that the US and NATO would not expand eastward, and that President Bush, Thatcher, Kohl and NATO all agreed that NATO would "not move an inch to the east", and that on the basis of this agreement Soviet forces withdrew from Eastern Europe, the Berlin Wall was breached and Germany was reunited. It was subsequently denied by Gorbachev that NATO's expansion was discussed or part of the agreement. (Steven Pifer, 'Did NATO Promise Not to Enlarge? Gorbachev Says "No"', https://www.brookings.edu/blog/up-front /2014/11/06/did-nato-promise-not-to-enlarge-gorbachev-says-no/.) Had I been able to visit Gorbachev, I could have asked him to confirm this.

In 1999 President Clinton expanded NATO eastwards and absorbed Poland, the Czech Republic and Hungary, and in 2004 President George W. Bush expanded NATO to the Russian border and absorbed

Bulgaria, Slovakia, Croatia and the Baltic states (Estonia, Latvia and Lithuania). Both Yeltsin and Putin had proposed that as it was no longer Communist, Russia should work in partnership with the US, and offered to discuss Russia's joining NATO and the EU.

Originally this may have been behind Putin's seeing a "common economic space" from Lisbon to Vladivostok in 2010 (see maps on pp.97 and 134). In 2008 the US pressured NATO to announce that Ukraine and Georgia would be the next for NATO membership. Putin said that this was a red line and that Russia would respond by retaking Crimea, which eventually happened, and meanwhile took military action in Georgia to prevent it from joining NATO.

Instead of replacing the Cold War with Gorbachev's vision of including Russia in the EU and NATO, the US Neocons conducted unipolar wars in Iraq, Afghanistan, Libya and Syria and expanded NATO to the east, creating the resentment that led to Putin invading the ancestral lands of Crimea and now Ukraine, and allying with China, Iran, India, Saudi Arabia, Brazil and South Africa.

The US's financial support for Ukraine has been eye-catching. In 2004, President George W. Bush gave $65 million to Ukraine to provide "democracy training" to opposition leaders and their activists, including paying Viktor Yushchenko (the third President of Ukraine from 23 January 2005 to 25 January 2010) to meet US leaders and help underwrite exit polls indicating he won disputed elections. The program was accelerated under President Barack Obama. In December 2013 as the Maidan Square protests escalated, Victoria Nuland confirmed that the US had invested "over $5 billion" (see p.76) to "ensure a secure and prosperous and democratic Ukraine", and she congratulated the Euromaidan movement.[21]

The US sent money and arms into Ukraine and encouraged it to join NATO and the EU after the discoveries of new deposits of natural gas in eastern Ukraine and under Ukraine's share of the Black Sea.

Since 24 February 2022, the date Russia invaded Ukraine, the US has poured money into Ukraine:

- Feb. 26: "Biden approves $350 million in military aid for Ukraine": Reuters;

- Mar. 16: "Biden announces $800 million in military aid for Ukraine": *The New York Times*;
- Mar. 30: "Ukraine to receive additional $500 million in aid from U.S., Biden announces": NBC News;
- Apr. 12: "U.S. to announce $750 million more in weapons for Ukraine, officials say": Reuters;
- May 6: "Biden announces new $150 million weapons package for Ukraine": Reuters.[22]

These amounts exceed $3 billion. In mid-March 2022 Congress authorised a further $13.5 billion, most of which was for weapons (and the US weapons industry). On 28 April 2022 it was announced that Biden's administration was asking for $33 billion in funding to respond to the Russian invasion of Ukraine – and Congress raised it to $40 billion, an increase of more than 20 per cent. House Speaker Nancy Pelosi said in a letter to House members that the amount would help Ukraine defend "democracy for the world". Some thought Biden cared more about Ukraine than the US, where almost 30 million Americans are without health insurance. There have been calls for a diplomatic solution to Ukraine from Noam Chomsky, Donald Trump and Henry Kissinger, but these have been isolated calls. The US gave Ukraine another $2.98 billion in military aid for weapons and equipment on 24 August 2022, the 31st anniversary of Ukraine's independence and to mark six months after the Russian invasion. (On the same day the UK gave a £54 million package of drones and munitions.)

On 18 September 2022 an article by Jeffrey Sachs appeared in *China Daily*. It began, "The war in Ukraine is the culmination of a 30-year project of the American neoconservative movement. The Biden Administration is packed with the same neocons who championed the US wars of choice in Serbia (1999), Afghanistan (2001), Iraq (2003), Syria (2011), Libya (2011), and who did so much to provoke Russia's conflict with Ukraine.... As a result Biden is steering Ukraine, the US and the EU towards yet another geopolitical debacle." The assumption is that Russia was deliberately pushed into an attack on Ukraine by America, rather than that Russia invaded Ukraine in a war of its choice.

This view (which was greeted with scepticism in the West) was supported in *Nya Dagbladet*, a Swedish online newspaper. On 13 September 2022 its editor Markus Andersson (markus.andersson@nyadagbladet.se) and managing editor Isac Boman (isac.boman@nyadagbladet.se) published an allegedly leaked Research Report marked Confidential for the American think-tank RAND Corporation, which was behind American strategy for foreign and defence policies during the Cold War and is now principally connected to the United States Department of Defense and the Pentagon. The document contains a detailed account of how the energy crisis in Europe was planned by the US.

The document is dated 25 January 2022, and the recipients listed are: the White House Chief of Staff; the US State Department; America's two primary intelligence services the Central Intelligence Agency (CIA) and the National Security Agency (NSA); and the Democratic National Committee (DNC), the Democratic Party's governing body.

The American document acknowledges Ukraine's aggressive foreign policy that would push Russia into taking military action against Ukraine. The purpose of this aggressive action was to pressure Europe into adopting a wide range of sanctions against Russia, which had already been prepared. As a result, the document states, the EU economy would collapse and resources of up to $9 billion would flow back into the US as young people in the EU would be forced to emigrate.

The main aim of the strategy was to weaken Germany, and the opening heading of the document is "Weakening Germany, strengthening the US". The document states: "Only European countries bound by EU and NATO commitments can provoke us with these [resources] without significant military and political costs for us." The growing independence of Germany had become a problem. Brexit had given Germany greater independence and made it more difficult for the US to influence the decisions of European governments.

The RAND document states that the American objective is to destroy the co-operation between Germany and Russia:

> Stopping Russian deliveries [of natural gas]... would be devastating for the German economy and inadvertently for the European Union as a whole. The only possible way to ensure that Germany rejects Russian

energy supplies is to draw both sides into the military conflict in Ukraine. Our continued actions in this country [Ukraine] will inevitably lead to a military response from Russia. Russia is clearly not going to leave [due] to the massive Ukrainian army's pressure on the Donetsk People's Republic without a military response. This would make it possible to portray Russia as the aggressive party and then implement the entire package of sanctions, which has already been drawn up.

RAND Corporation denies originating the Report, and the former Prime Minister of Sweden rejects the RAND leak as falsified. The Report's authenticity was being debated. The Swedish political analyst Stig Berglund said it did not seem fake or disinformation as it followed RAND's existing strategic line.

At the Western summit at Ramstein Air Base on 20 January 2023, Germany was pressurised to allow German Leopard-2 tanks to be sent to Ukraine. The UK had announced it would donate a squadron of 14 Challenger-2 tanks to Ukraine, the US said it would send 31 M1 Abrams tanks (which run on jet fuel) and spare parts besides sending missiles, and Germany belatedly announced it would send a squadron of 14 Leopard-2 tanks and lift the ban on other countries, including Poland, re-exporting their Leopard-2 tanks to Ukraine to help Ukraine's armed forces reclaim territory. Ukraine's NATO allies hold 2,000 Leopard-2 tanks (viewed as the world's fastest and most reliable) and could collectively send hundreds of these to Ukraine. It would take months for these to be sent to Ukraine: the American Abrams tanks were thought to be set to arrive in August 2023, long after Russia's spring offensive. Ukraine needed hundreds of tanks, and only about 150 were committed. The Russians called the decision a "dangerous escalation".

It looked as if the war was being escalated from a war about Russia's invasion of Ukraine into a proxy Third World War of weaponry, with the West and NATO (the US, UK, Germany and allies) sending weapons to fight Russian weapons, and it looked as if a step-by-step approach to a Third World War had started. Now that Germany had been successfully separated from Russia, it looked as if weaponry might be followed by Western troops trained to use their weapons expertly. The secretary-general of the EU's external action service, Stefano Sannino, said that Russia is now engaged in "a war against NATO and the West" – a step closer to a Third World War. In February 2023 Russian warships armed with tactical nuclear weapons steamed into the Baltic, threatening NATO according to Norwegian intelligence, another step towards a Third World War. Some feared the escalation would end in a nuclear war.

Ukraine's aggression towards Russia that was supported in the alleged RAND leak can be connected to another leak of Ukrainian documents. The Australian NEXUSNewsfeed.com on 17 September 2022 drew attention to allegedly leaked documents that exposed Ukraine's attempts to destabilise Russia and draw NATO into a full-scale war with Moscow. An ex-Ukrainian diplomat, Olga Sukharevskaya, drawing on a Russian source at rt.com, presented plans set out by the Ukrainian special services that reveal Kyiv's aggressive strategy over eight years.

In June 2022 a hacker Telegram channel, 'Beregini', had published an action plan devised in 2017 by the Information and Psychological Operations Department of the Armed Forces of Ukraine's Special Operations Forces (SSO) to create networks of agents, infiltrate, conduct espionage and destroy threats to the Ukrainian government. Operation 'Zasion' was to influence the family members of Donbas soldiers and militiamen; Operation 'Bolotnaya Square' sowed distrust of Russia's military and political leaders; Operation 'Steppe Wind' was to create tension between the Russian military and fighters in Donbas and Luhansk; Operation 'Gentle Dew' was aimed at territories not controlled by Ukraine; Operation 'Caspian' sowed discord between the Russian Federation and countries in the Caspian region; and Operation 'Manchurian Hills' aimed to worsen Russia's diplomatic relations with the countries in the Far East.

All these Operations were part of a Ukrainian strategy to present Russia's actions as an attack by a Great Power on a small state, and may have riled Putin since they were put into practice in 2017, and may have contributed to American support for Ukraine's aggressive actions.

It seems that America has wanted to continue to be a unipolar power, the only superpower, and that at an early stage of the war in Ukraine the US dissuaded Zelensky from talking to the Russians, having in mind a future of Europe in which the US was still sole superpower, as in 1991 after the collapse of the Soviet Union and breach of the Berlin Wall.

On 21 March 2020 Biden's spokesman Ned Price, asked what he was saying about his support for "a negotiated settlement à la Zelensky", replied: "This is a war that is in many ways bigger than Russia, it's bigger than Ukraine." (See Ted Snider, ZeroHedge, 26 November 2022, 'It Was Never About Ukraine', https://www.zerohedge.com/geopolitical/it-was-never-about-ukraine.) In other words the war was to keep the US as the sole unipolar superpower in relation to Russia, China and the rest of the world.

In his speech of 24 February, Putin referred to his attempt in December 2021 to ensure "the non-expansion of NATO", but "in vain". (His attempt was actually Russian demands, as we saw on p.65.) He complained of being deceived after being promised that NATO would not expand "one inch to the east". He described the "Western bloc, formed by the United States in its own image and likeness", as "the very 'empire of lies'". His "special military operation" could have meant putting right the consequences of American intervention in eastern Ukraine.

But there is an even more sinister threat that the "special military operation" was trying to demolish.

US biological laboratories in Ukraine

In *The Fall of the West* I set out[23] how the US did gain-of-function research work in the US from 1999, especially at the University of North Carolina, and that when President Obama banned it in the US in 2013, Dr Fauci and others took the research to Wuhan and continued it at the Wuhan Institute of Virology until President Trump allowed it to resume in the US in 2017. There is some evidence that the US also took gain-of-function research, making viruses more dangerous by making them more airborne, stick to lungs and damage immune systems, to Ukraine, and that there were 23, or even 30, biological laboratories in Ukraine that represented a biological-warfare threat to Russia; and that the "special military operation" was to hunt these down and eliminate the biological threat.

On 8 March 2022 Victoria Nuland, US Under Secretary of State for Political Affairs since 2021, a neocon, testified before the Senate Foreign Relations Committee and was asked by Republican Senator of Florida Marco Rubio, "Does Ukraine have chemical or biological weapons?" He was undoubtedly expecting a denial and was stunned when Nuland said, "Uh, Ukraine has, uh, biological research facilities. We are now quite concerned that Russian troops, Russian forces, may be seeking to, uh, gain control of [those laboratories] so we are working with the Ukrainiahhns [*sic*] on how they can prevent any of those research materials from falling into the hands of Russian forces should they approach."[24]

The Chinese Foreign Ministry claimed in March 2022, "The US has 336 labs in 30 countries under its control, including 26 in Ukraine alone." The Russian Foreign Ministry claimed that "Russia obtained documents proving that Ukrainian biological laboratories located near Russian borders worked on development of components of biological weapons". These assertions, and the denials of US fact-checkers who claim that they are "disinformation", deserve to be treated with scepticism, but following Nuland's admission they must feature in the evidence as pieces of the jigsaw to be assembled to give a picture of why Putin invaded Ukraine.

The existence of a Ukrainian biological research program, perhaps with American-supplied gain-of-function research, does not justify a Russian invasion on its own, but it may contribute to the threat Russia clearly felt to the Russian-speaking statelets in the Donbas, Donetsk and Luhansk. Russian researchers may already have all the viruses being explored in Ukraine, but the American concern would be if the US had made available sophisticated materials in Ukraine that Russian scientists had not developed on their own, which could be taken back to Russia and used against the West.

Nuland's worry that the research materials in Ukraine might fall into the hands of the Russian forces suggests that the US assisted in the construction and development of "the biological research facilities", which are fundamentally American. The US Embassy in Ukraine publicly boasted of its collaborative work with Ukraine "to consolidate and secure pathogens and toxins of security concern and to continue to ensure Ukraine can detect and report outbreaks caused by dangerous pathogens before they pose security or stability threats".[25]

It goes without saying that "defensive" research such as that done in the course of strengthening coronavirus, which was funded by the Pentagon,[26] can easily be converted into offensive and destructive biological weapons.

Russia's Permanent Representative to the UN's evidence to the Security Council on biological weapons

Vassily Nebenzia, Permanent Representative of Russia to the UN, made a statement to the 15-member UN Security Council at the UN Security Council's briefing on biological laboratories in Ukraine on 11 March 2022.[27] He said that the Ministry of Defence of the Russian Federation have documents confirming that Ukraine developed 30 biological laboratories that host dangerous biological experiments to enhance the pathogen properties of plague, anthrax, tularaemia, cholera, and other lethal diseases. The work was funded and directly supervised by the Defense Threat Reduction Agency (DTRA) of the US. This means it was in the interests (like the Pentagon-funded coronavirus gain-of-function work in Wuhan and the US) of the Pentagon's National Center for Medical Intelligence.

The key role was in a BSL-3 (Bio-Safety Level 3) central research laboratory at the Mechnikov Scientific-Research Anti-Plague Institute in Odesa, Ukraine. There were research centres in other cities: Kyiv, Lvov, Kharkov, Dnipro, Kherson, Ternopol, Uzhgorod and Vinnytsia. Research results were sent to the US Army Medical Research Institute of Infectious Diseases, Walter Reed Army Institute of Research, US Naval Medical Research, and US Army Biological Warfare Laboratories in Fort Detrick, that all used to be centres for the American biological weapons program.

The Ukrainian UP-4 project at laboratories in Kyiv, Kharkov and Odesa studied spreading dangerous infections through migratory birds, including highly pathogenic H5N1 influenza (which is lethal to humans in 50 per cent of cases) and the Newcastle disease virus (NDV), an infection of domestic poultry. In another project bats were considered as carriers for biological-warfare agents: bacterial and viral pathogens (plague, leptospirosis, brucellosis, coronaviruses and filoviruses) that can be transmitted from bats to humans. There were also experiments to spread dangerous infectious diseases by ectoparasites (fleas and lice). UP-4 project documents clearly show that the US actively financed biological projects in Ukraine.

Many bird migration routes pass from Ukraine through Russia and Eastern Europe, and ringed birds released from the Kherson nature reserve during biological research were caught in the Ivanovo and Voronezh regions of Russia. One hundred and forty containers with bats' fleas and lice from a biological laboratory in Kharkov were found abroad.

Activities in biological laboratories in Ukraine can be tracked back to 2014, soon after US President Obama banned research in the USA, because of the risks to the American population, in 2013. In Kharkov 20 Ukrainian soldiers died of swine flu in January 2016, and 200 were hospitalised. After Obama banned military-purpose biological research within the USA, the Kyiv authorities agreed to turn Ukraine into a biological testing site and to allow its citizens to be used as test subjects.

The WHO (World Health Organization) recommended that Ukraine should eliminate its stocks of pathogens to avoid leaks that might infect the Ukrainian population. Article 1 of the UN's Biological Weapons Convention states that never under any circumstances can a nation-state develop, produce, stockpile and acquire or retain biological weapons, and the Biological and Toxic Weapons Convention (BTWC) mandates the elimination of existing biological weapons and prohibits developing, stockpiling or using biological and toxin weapons.

Blood serum taken from Slavic people under the pretext of curing Covid was allegedly sent to the Walter Reed Army Institute of Research in the US, and these samples were linked to biological agents that can selectively target specific ethnic groups.[28]

Ukraine's Health Ministry ordered that biological agents deposited in Ukrainian biological laboratories should be eliminated, starting from 24 February 2022 (the date of Russia's invasion of Ukraine). In the Lvov biological laboratory 232 containers with pathogens of leptospirosis were destroyed, 30 of tularaemia, 10 of brucellosis and 5 of plague. The elimination of more than 320 containers, the diseases they harboured and their quantities suggests they were part of a military biological program.

Further briefing by Russian Defence Ministry on biological weapons in Ukraine

A further briefing from the Ministry of Defence of the Russian Federation was released on 11 May 2022. More than two-and-a-half months after Russia's invasion of Ukraine, this briefing reports on the invasion force's findings regarding military biological programs of the US and its NATO allies implemented within Ukraine. The briefing's reference to "biological weapons" includes pathogenic micro-organisms and toxins and the means of delivering them. The briefing states that "as a result of the special military operation on the territory of Ukraine, facts of work with the specified pathogens, which are political agents of biological weapons, have been revealed". The use of "special military operation" seems to confirm that a principal aim of the Russian invasion of Ukraine was to hunt these pathogens down.[29]

The briefing states that Ukraine had sent a request to the manufacturing company of Bayraktar drones asking if it was possible to fit the drones with aerosol equipment. Three unmanned aerial vehicles were found equipped with 30-litre containers in Kherson region on 9 March 2022, and 10 more were found near Kakhovka on 10 April 2022. It was previously found that Ukraine had been a testing ground for the development of biological weapons, and the ideologues for this approach in Ukraine had now been found to be the leaders of the US Democratic Party.

Funding for military biomedical research had been raised from funds controlled by the Democratic-Party leadership, including the investment funds of the Clintons, 'Rockefellers', Soros, and Biden, and the scheme involved pharmaceutical companies including Pfizer, Moderna, Merck and Gilead. Pentagon contractors and Ukrainian State agencies were involved in military bioweapons activities. Twelve countries, including Germany and Ukraine, were involved in the program.

Between 2016 and 2019 3,500 blood-serum samples taken from Ukrainian citizens living in 25 regions of Ukraine were removed by military epidemiologists from the Bundeswehr Microbiology Institute, which raises questions about the goals of the German armed forces in collecting biomaterials of Ukrainian citizens. The Polish Institute of Veterinary Medicine had been assessing the spread of the rabies virus in Ukraine in research carried out jointly with the US-based Battelle Institute, a key contractor for the Pentagon. There had been Polish funding for the Lvov Medical University's Institute of Epidemiology and Hygiene, which includes a number of US military biology projects.

The "special military operation" by Russian troops obtained information indicating the intentional use in 2020 of a multi-drug-resistant tuberculosis pathogen to infect the people of the Slavyanoserbsky district of the Russian-speaking Luhansk People's Republic. Counterfeit currency notes were infected with the tuberculosis agent and distributed to young people in Stepovoe village.

There were trials of potentially-dangerous biological drugs on patients of the Kharkov Regional Clinical Psychiatric Hospital no.3. There were details of the Pentagon's experiments on Ukrainian citizens (physically-exhausted males aged between 40 and 60) in Psychiatric Hospital no.1 in Streleche village in the Kharkov region.

Russian Defence Ministry specialists have carried out work in two biolaboratories in Mariupol, where documentation indicates that Mariupol was a regional centre for cholera pathogen collection and certification. From 2014 on, the selected strains were sent to the Public Health Centre in Kyiv, and from there they were shipped to the US. Cholera, tularaemia and anthrax pathogens were destroyed on 25 February 2022 in the sanitary and epidemiological laboratory in Mariupol. Part of the collection of typhoid, paratyphoid and gas gangrene in the veterinary laboratory in Mariupol was not destroyed, and 124 strains were sent to Russia for safe and secure storage. The presence of these pathogens in a veterinary laboratory suggests that it was involved in a military biological program.

The Ukrainian Ministry of Health in Kyiv asked the US to send equipment for personal skin and respiratory protection against toxic chemicals and biological contaminating agents. The US sent 220,000 ampoules of atropine in 2022, and preparations for special treatment and disinfection.

The Ministry of Defence of the Russian Federation maintains that all the above information confirms that the US was implementing an offensive military-biological program in Ukraine to study releasing controlled epidemics in specific Russian-occupied territories in Ukraine.

The briefing concludes that the "special military operation" of the Russian armed forces has crossed and stopped the US military-biological expansion in Ukraine and has stopped criminal experiments on civilians.

Vassily Nebenzia, the Permanent Representative of Russia to the UN, has subsequently given the UN Security Council (UNSC) volumes of evidence spanning eight months, and on 29 October 2022 the UNSC debated the possible enactment of Article 6 of the Biological and Toxic Weapons Convention (BTWC) to investigate the US's biolab in Ukraine. This debate was triggered by a complain lodged on 24 October 2022 that the US and Ukraine had violated the BTWC in Ukraine. Joe Biden had been in charge of Ukraine policy for the US administration, and his son Hunter Biden had joined the board of Burisma Holdings Ltd, a Ukrainian gas company in 2014 while his father was Vice-President (*The Sunday Times*, 20 November 2022). There were unsubstantiated allegations about Hunter Biden's personal involvement in Ukrainian laboratories and his attracting funds for Black and Veatch and Metabiota companies to finance deadly pathogens: drones with aerosol canisters to dispense airborne water particles containing pathogens, and the aerial release of many infected mosquitoes. A UNSC letter about it (S/2022/796) was circulated on 25 October 2022.

Russia expected a report from the UNSC "no later than November 30, 2022", when the Ninth Review Conference of the Biological Weapons Treaty (28 November–16 December 2022) would have begun. Russia conducted its allegations via diplomatic channels and presented its case in a convincing manner, whereas the US and NATO dismissed the allegations as "disinformation" without engaging in them.

All the above evidence came from first the Russian representative to the UN and then from the Ministry of Defence of the Russian Federation. I have set out the allegations in full as the 11-May follow-up to the 11-March evidence was specifically presented to the UN as being the reason for the "special military operation" in Ukraine on 24 February 2022. The other 14 members of the UN Security Council did not accept the 11-March evidence, some following the US lead in denying the existence of biological laboratories in Ukraine. There is no proof, and the 'evidence' may have been presented to justify Russia's invasion of Ukraine; and may understandably be treated with caution.

Some Russian biologists have said that the documents presented by the Ministry of Defence of the Russian Federation referred to harmless collections of pathogens for public health research.[30] But it does fit in with the picture the evidence is giving, of US gain-of-function research outside the USA after 2013. It all fits: new deposits of natural gas found in eastern Ukraine and under Ukraine's share of the Black Sea in 2012; the deal with 'Rothschildite' Royal Dutch Shell to drill in eastern Ukraine in 2013; the organised impeachment of Yanukovych in 2014; and biological research being moved to Wuhan around this time, and also to Ukraine. Because the above evidence came from Russia does not mean it must automatically be discredited, just treated with caution.

Russia's dream of its own New World Order

Why, then, did the invasion of Ukraine happen? So far we have considered: Russia's natural-gas routes through Ukraine, Russia's nationalistic history and the need for "demilitarisation and denazification", and the idea that biological laboratories in Ukraine might be the reason for the "special military operation". According to Ukrainian intelligence, reported in the *Kyiv Independent* on 2 March 2022, Putin wanted to reinstate President Yanukovych.[31]

There is another consideration: Russia's political dream of its own world order. On 24 February 2022 US State Department spokesman Ned Price stated that "Russia and the PRC [People's Republic of China] also [i.e. besides the US] want a world order. But this is an order that is and would be profoundly illiberal."[32] He was saying that the Russia-Ukraine war would determine who will rule the coming world order. He tacitly admitted that the US and Western nations desire to have a world order of their own, which will be liberal, and he implied that there is a battle over whether the US or Russia and China will run the new "world order".

Putin in his speech on 24 February 2022 said, "Whoever has to impede us… must know that the Russian response will be immediate and lead to consequences you have never seen in history." This seemed to suggest a Russian nuclear strike.

In an editorial by state news agency Ria-Novosti on 26 February 2022, then tellingly deleted, Putin praised a New World Order in which Russia was restoring its pre-1991 Soviet unity, gathering the Russian world of Russians, Belorussians and Little Russians (Ukrainians). This New World Order corresponds to the thinking in Putin's July 2021 historical essay, 'On the Historical Unity of Russians and Ukrainians', which described Russians and Ukrainians as one nation (see p.99). Putin has described the collapse of the Soviet Union in December 1991 as the "disintegration of historical Russia".

On 21 March 2022 President Biden alluded to a coming "new world order" during a gathering of business leaders at the White House. Addressing the Business Roundtable's CEO Quarterly Meeting, which included the bosses of General Motors, Apple and Amazon, he concluded his remarks by saying: "Now is a time when things are shifting. We're going to – there's going to be a new world order out there, and we've got to lead it. And we've got to unite the rest of the free world in doing it."[33]

What would Russia's new world order be? As I said on p.80 it would involve Russia's seizure of the Donbas region, including

Putin's vision in 2010 of a "common economic space" stretching from Lisbon to Vladivostok and including the European Union, Russia and the UK – all within a new Russian world order?

Donetsk and Luhansk (as has happened). It could connect up with Moldova and Transnistria, absorb the Ukrainian territory through which the Russian Soyuz and Brotherhood pipelines pass, and go on to Poland and from there win back the countries lost by Gorbachev, the former Soviet Eastern Europe. Putin's ideal, expressed in 2010, is of a "common economic space" between Lisbon and Vladivostok (see map on p.97), and that would involve the conquest of Western Europe. For Putin's vision expressed in a German newspaper in 2010 may not be of an enlarged European Union, but of a Russian New World Order that includes the European Union.

Putin may have been thinking that the Russian Empire of the Tsars should be enlarged to extend from Lisbon to Vladivostok. This would be the beginning of a Russian New World Order, and a Third World War would be looming if Putin were to pursue this narrative. Hence Putin's strong insistence, his demand in December 2021, that Ukraine has nothing to do with NATO or the EU.

Putin compares himself to Peter the Great as a taker-back of Russian lands

At an exhibition in Moscow marking the 350th anniversary of the birth of the 18th-century Tsar Peter the Great, who founded St Petersburg, on 9 June 2022 Putin addressed a group of young entrepreneurs and scientists and compared the war in Ukraine to Peter the Great's conquests in the Baltic, and compared his historic quest to win back Ukrainian lands to Peter the Great's winning back of lands from Sweden. He argued that in both conflicts Russia was recovering its territory. He said of Peter the Great, "Peter the Great waged the northern war for 21 years. It seemed he was at war with Sweden and took something from them…. He did not take anything from them, he returned [what was Russia's]."

He went on to imply that swathes of Ukrainian lands would soon be annexed and reclaimed in the same way: "When Peter the Great laid the foundation of a new capital in St Petersburg, none of the European countries recognised this territory as Russian, everyone recognised it as Swedish. But along with Finno-Ugric peoples, Slavs lived there from ancient times. Why did he invade it? To reclaim [our lands] and strengthen [the state].... It's our turn now to return [the lands of Ukraine] and strengthen [the state]." He meant that the same task had fallen to him today, because (translating the Russian slightly differently): "It is our responsibility also to take back and strengthen."[34]

In July 2021 the Kremlin published a historic essay by Putin, 'On the Historical Unity of Russians and Ukrainians', in which he argued that Russia and Ukraine were one nation, artificially divided (see p.97). This essay again suggests that Putin's decision to invade Ukraine was taken before March 2021. In his pre-dawn speech on 24 February 2022, before the Russian invasion of Ukraine, Putin blamed Lenin for creating Ukraine on Russian territory, and praised Stalin for his "tightly centralised and absolutely unitary state".

The exhibition in Moscow was named 'Peter I: The Birth of an Empire', and he was implying that like Peter the Great he was bringing to birth an empire that was signalled in the Mayan Year of the Phoenix's reappearance after 2,000 years. Peter the Great's crown, orb and sceptre were the key exhibits in the Diamond Depository (see p.55), and provided a clue to Putin's territorial ambitions. Putin's complaints about eastward NATO expansion and threats from America may have been a façade for a traditional war of conquest, like Peter's capturing of lands Sweden had annexed from the Polish-Ukrainian Commonwealth. Peter the Great also controlled most of the Gulf of Finland and modern Estonia as well as the site of what would become St Petersburg, and Finland and Estonia could be future targets for Putin.[35]

It was also reported in June 2022 that children at nurseries and schools (for example, in Chita in eastern Siberia) were being dressed in uniforms with 'Z' (the symbol for the Russian invasion of Ukraine displayed on tanks) on their left-hand breast pockets and in flat caps to sing a 2014 song, 'Uncle Vova [short for Vladimir], We Are With You', whose chorus says: "From the northern seas to the southern borders, from the Kurile islands to the Baltic coast, on this earth there would be peace, but if the chief commander calls [us] to the last battle, Uncle Vova, we are with you." The children were being prepared for death (their last battle).

The lyrics promise to maintain Russia's role in Crimea and return "to the motherland" Alaska, which Tsarist Russia sold to the US in the 19th century. Russian schools were ordered to hold special lessons explaining that Russia was forced to invade Ukraine to defend people in the Donbas region from "Nazis" and to ensure that Kyiv does not become a platform for an attack on Russia by NATO.[36]

It is clear from Putin's words about Peter the Great and the lyrics Russian children in uniform were being asked to sing in praise of Putin (which reminds me of watching schoolchildren sing in praise of Chairman Mao in Peking [Beijing] in 1966) that a key reason for Russia's invasion of Ukraine was to return or take back Russian lands.

If all countries were allowed by international law to return or take back their previously owned territories to be once again under their rule, then Hungary would take back a western slice of Ukraine that once belonged to the Austro-Hungarian Empire; Turkey would take back the countries that once belonged to the Ottoman Empire, including Syria; China would take back lands it used to own to the west under the Han Empire; Mongolia would take back its former Mughal territories; the Polish-Lithuanian Commonwealth would take back its former European territories; and England would take back a northern part of France it ruled in the 14th and 15th centuries. The plains of eastern Ukraine were at different times occupied by nomadic horsemen: the Yamnaya of 3300–2600BC, then the Scythians, then the Mongols and then the Cossacks, all of whom, if international law allowed, could return and take back bits of Ukraine.

It has to be said that Putin's thinking of returning Ukraine to Russian rule, if seen in the light of the above possible returners or takers-back, is unacceptable, and if applied universally would leave the world in permanent warfare and chaos – the opposite of the peaceful democratic World State I outlined to my audience two miles from the Kremlin in 2019. Having written two letters to Putin (see pp.12–14 and 35–38) I feel it may be appropriate to urge him now to abandon nationalism, which always leads to war, and drop his taking-back of past Russian lands and work with me supranationally for a democratic World State that will bring in a universal peace and disarmament, in accordance with what I said in Moscow on 22 April 2019.

Putin's nuclear threat

Russia's former president from 2008 to 2012 while Putin was term-limited, Dmitri Medvedev, said on 12 May 2022 that NATO countries sending weapons into Ukraine, training Ukrainian troops to use Western equipment, and sending mercenaries for exercises in NATO countries near Russia's borders increased the likelihood of a direct and open conflict between NATO and Russia. He said, "Such a conflict always has the risk of turning into a fully-fledged nuclear war." He also said, "The horsemen of the apocalypse are already on their way."[37]

Putin's nuclear threat to Europe and the UK is from his RS-28 Sarmat, known as Satan II, or 2: a hypersonic intercontinental ballistic missile with a range of 18,000 kms (11,000 miles) that travels at 25,500 kms per hour (15,844 mph) and would take two-and-a-half minutes to reach the UK, with 10 heavy or 15 light MIRV (multiple independently targetable re-entry vehicle) warheads, that separate to target different places as separate nuclear weapons, working like a cluster bomb. It could devastate an area the size of France or Texas.

This would mean that if it were dropped on Birmingham in the UK, the whole of the UK would be wiped out. Or, as a commentator on Russian state television put it of the UK on 2 May 2022, "The island is so small that one Sarmat missile is enough to drown it once and for all. The Russian missile Sarmat, the world's most powerful... is capable of... destroying an area the size of Texas or England. A single launch, Boris, and there is no England any more. Once and for all." He said that Britain will be hit with a "radioactive tidal wave" after a Russian nuclear attack on the Atlantic Ocean just west of Ireland.[38]

In *The Fall of the West* I described the depopulation predictions of the US's most secret intelligence agency, Deagel.com, from 2025: the US down from 327 million to just under 100 million, the UK down from 66 million to 15 million; Germany down from 81 million to 28 million; and France down from 67 million to 39 million.[39] Deagel's disclaimer written in 2020 suggests the world will experience "the first nuclear war".[40] Deagel.com seems to know in advance what will happen and in 2022 we can see how these reduced population figures could take place, if Russia were to unleash RS-28 Sarmats.

Covid as a population reducer

There may be another reason for Deagel.com's forecast of world population reduction. I described the Great Reset after the pandemic (see p.4), and as we shall see on p.105 the Great Reset blurs the distinction between the physical, digital and biological worlds. It is possible that the vaccination program for Covid may be part of a Syndicate World Health Organization population reduction program.

In *The Fall of the West* I showed that US researchers Anthony Fauci and Ralph Baric were working on coronavirus since 1999,[41] and I wrote of David Martin, whose company M-CAM is the world's largest underwriter of intangible assets used in finance in 168 countries and monitored biological and chemical weapons treaty violations on behalf of the US government. In an interview with Joseph Mercola,[42] Martin spoke of 4,000 patents relating to SARS coronavirus. Now that story has developed, with Martin describing the Pfizer and Moderna vaccines as manufacturing spike protein in the body and turning the body into a biological weapons factory.[43]

Fauci and Baric patented coronavirus in 2002,[44] and then began weaponising coronavirus the year before the SARS outbreak in China. Martin claims they knew their gain-of-function weaponising of coronavirus was a bioweapon from 2005, and that it could reduce populations. In 2011 the World Health Organization announced a "decade of vaccination" in a collaboration with stakeholders: the Bill and Melinda Gates Foundation, the Chinese Center for Disease Control and Prevention, the Jeremy Farrar Wellcome Trust and others, who developed the idea for the World Health Organization's immunisation strategy and Global Vaccine Action Plan. A 2010 TED talk appeared to give the impression that Bill Gates had a plan to remove some of the world population through vaccines, to enforce population reduction through forced vaccines, but FactCheck have found this to be false.

Martin says their stated objective was a population reduction of 15 per cent of the world's population: about 700 million people, including 75–100 million Americans, by 2028, to control the world's population and keep it below 8 billion. In fact, the world population reached 8 billion in November 2022. He believes that the vaccination program has implemented this policy as the spike protein the vaccine manufactures is a computer simulation of a chimera of the spike protein of coronavirus. He claims it is an instruction to make the body produce a toxin. In 2015 Baric, who collaborated with Shi Zhengli in the Wuhan Institute of Virology from 2013, published a paper that stated that the Wuhan Institute of Virology SARS-like WIV1-CoV virus was "poised for human emergence", by which time it had been patented 73 times.[45] In *The Fall of the West* I describe how the Pentagon and State Department funded the coronavirus research with $103 million from 2013 to 2020.[46]

Martin now believes that population control was behind vaccinating over-65s first, and that those compulsorily vaccinated, such as pilots, are now unwell, and that 700 flights a day have been cancelled as pilots have developed microvascular problems which have made them prone to clots, strokes and heart attacks. Martin has drawn attention to a little-known grant from the National Science Foundation, known as Darwinian Chemical Systems, which involved research to incorporate mRNA into targeted genomes. This is speculative.

On a personal note, I was found to have perimyocarditis and an infected heart muscle, tachycardia and arrhythmia four months after having extremely mild Covid in November 2021, so mild that I did not realise I had it while being interviewed on Zoom by Paula Vail for American TV, at the end of which she asked me to sign copies of my *World State* and *World Constitution* to President Biden, and send them to her so she could personally give them to him, which I did (see p.153).

My perimyocarditis has now receded into the past, controlled and overcome by medication, and I would say that my two Covid jabs and two boosters protected me from highly dangerous Covid and that Covid – which may be a weaponised disease – did (perhaps gain-of-function) things in my heart and lung areas during the next four months. I could say from personal experience that there is no truth that Covid vaccination was intended to be a cull. On the contrary, all I encountered within the system were doing their best to prevent me from succumbing to Covid. The question of whether there has been a population reduction program through the World Health Organization is unproved.

In view of this conclusion, it is likely that Deagel.com's world population reduction forecast was based on a nuclear attack on the West, and not on a forced Covid vaccination program.

Russian and Syndicate New World Orders

So defending natural gas from Ukrainian competition, de-Westernising Ukraine, reducing NATO's extent, and eliminating American biological laboratories alleged to be in Ukraine now all seem part of a commercial-political strategy to extend Russia's nationalistic influence by taking back lands and to make possible a Russian authoritarian New World Order it would share with China.

When I spoke in Moscow to an audience that included men in military uniform on 22 April 2019 and described a "democratic World State", the military men may have been replacing my word 'democratic' with the word 'Russian' in their minds (as I suggested on p.81) and seeing a World State ahead that will get back lands that have been appropriated and exploited by Russia's traditional enemies, in the case of Ukraine by Ukrainians and their Western military and political allies and commercial partners who are helping Ukraine to become Russia's competitor in supplying the European Union with natural gas.

But lurking behind all this is the international nature of the Western Syndicate's New World Order, to which Ned Price referred on 24 February 2022 with his word 'also'. With 'Rockefellers' and 'Rothschilds' in alliance within the Syndicate but individually backing opposite sides ('Rockefellers' backing Russia and Gazprom, 'Rothschilds' backing Ukraine and Royal Dutch Shell) the Western Syndicate's New World Order is levelling down the West and levelling up the East to achieve a balance.

The sanctions on two-thirds of Russian natural gas by the 'Rothschildian' EU and UK carry forward 'Rothschilds'' competition with Russia for Ukraine's natural gas, and 'Rockefellerite' Gazprom announced on 1 June 2022 that in retaliation it would stop supplying natural gas to the Dutch company Gasterra, the largest gas trader in the Netherlands, owned by 'Rothschildian' Shell, Esso Nederland and the Dutch government. This announcement followed Gasterra's declining to pay for Russian gas in roubles to avoid violating the EU's sanctions against Russia, and would mean opening bank accounts in Moscow which would be risky as they would fall under Russian law.[47]

The Great Reset and Putin

There is another consideration as to why Russia invaded Ukraine on 24 February 2022: the invasion advanced the Great Reset. For as a result of the invasion, Russian natural gas was blocked by the EU, and Europe's and the world's energy is undergoing a change from oil- and gas-sourced to green-sourced. This is what Schwab of the World Economic Forum wanted,[48] and the Secretary-General of the UN, António Guterres, who has signed an agreement with Schwab to advance the 17 Sustainable Goals of the UN's Agenda 2030 in what[49] is called 'The Strategic Partnership Framework'.

I described the Great Reset in *The Fall of the West*. I said the Guterres-Schwab agenda involves the planned collapse of the West's GDP and financial system, and the replacement of shareholder capitalism by "stakeholder capitalism" in which the power of corporations is increased as they become the custodians of society and deliver the 17 Sustainable Goals of Agenda 2030, which will reduce the undeveloped world's population by at least 90 per cent.[50]

I said the Great Reset is technocratic and is blurring the dividing lines between the physical, digital and biological worlds. By blurring the distinction between human beings and the artificial intelligence of robots and machines, it will treat humans as machines, quietly remove their ownership so (in Schwab's words) "you will own nothing and you will be happy".

I said the Great Reset originated with the Syndicate, and is a rebranding of the coming Western New World Order. By including negative, abusive technocratic brain control, digitalising money to make 'Rothschildian' central banking supreme, building automated 'smart cities' which may also be 'eco-cities', and by removing ownership from the masses so only the corporations they work for own, the Great Reset will deliver a world that is a combination of *A Brave New World* and *1984*. It will advance the fall of the West so a levelled-down West and levelled-up East can meet in a New World Order. I said it needed to exploit a catastrophic incident: Covid. And now Ukraine has come along, another catastrophic incident.

Schwab, the Executive Chairman of the World Economic Forum (WEF), has known Putin for many years. In fact, their relationship dates back to 1982. After Schwab's annual gathering in Davos from 23 to 26 May 2022, St Petersburg International Economic Forum met in St Petersburg, the home of Gazprom, from 15 to 18 June 2022. Putin and his predecessor Medvedev addressed the WEF five times between 2007 and 2021.

Schwab meeting Putin in St Petersburg on 27 November 2019.

In 2019 Schwab met Putin in St Petersburg, and Putin said, "We have always maintained relations with your forum that you founded and we will continue to support it." Schwab noted that the WEF and Russia had had a high level of co-operation for many years. He said, "It has always been important for me that Russian representatives take part in our events in Davos." He said his goal was "to strengthen co-operation between business people and government agencies" so "climate and environmental problems" and "problems of economic growth" can be solved through co-operation "at the global level".[51] In January 2021 Schwab said that Putin's voice is "essential" in world affairs.

But following Russia's invasion of Ukraine, Schwab suspended his relationship with Russia and complied with US, EU and Swiss sanctions against Russia, which includes cutting ties with Russian banks and oil companies. The Russian House at Davos became the Russian War Crimes House and housed an exhibition on Russian war crimes in Ukraine.

It seems as if the split is genuine, but their previous closeness, and the fact that (we are being led to believe) the war in Ukraine is 'fortuitously' having an effect on the supply of gas and oil, which

Schwab has long desired and has been trying to reduce as part of the Great Reset, makes one wonder whether there was a plan in 2021 for Russia to deliver a situation in Ukraine that would enable the Great Reset to change the world's approach to energy and also the export of food. A greener world is what both Schwab and Guterres want, and amid attacks on Ukrainian civilians and their homes, oil and gas are being made more scarce, and this has started to happen.

It is theoretically possible that Putin and Gazprom are ultimately in league with the WEF and Western Syndicate. In view of the intensity and ruthlessness of the missile-flattening of residential apartments in Ukraine it realistically looks unlikely that Putin is collaborating with the West to advance the Great Reset at the expense of Russian oil and natural gas. Was he lured into Ukraine by Western misinformation? This is unlikely. Was he provoked, and did he just decide to go in for the reasons I have set out regarding natural gas, perhaps under the misapprehension that the war would be over in a few days? That is the most likely scenario. In that case, in the event Schwab and the West have taken advantage of the situation to advance their Great-Reset agenda.

The World Economic Forum and Putin's decision to invade Ukraine
We have seen (on p.75) that in 2012 two new deposits of natural gas were found in eastern Ukraine and under Ukraine's share of the Black Sea, and that in 2013 Ukraine needed an agreement with 'Rothschildite' Royal Dutch Shell to start drilling in eastern Ukraine. This was the provocation that brought Russia into Ukraine in 2022, as we have seen, and it is likely that Russia went in to see off Ukraine's attempt to be a net exporter of oil at Russia's expense. The World Economic Forum's support for Ukraine could have helped precipitate Russia's invasion, which the WEF turned to its advantage by implementing it as the next event in the post-Covid phase of the Great Reset.

On 23 May 2022 at Davos the President of the World Economic Forum Børge Brende called for a 'Marshall Plan' for the reconstruction in Ukraine. In other words, he called for the US to set up a huge fund of the kind it set up after the Second World War, that would finance and implement the Great Reset from Ukraine. President Zelensky of

Ukraine called for a fund to rebuild Ukraine and cited more than "half a trillion dollars of losses", with the urgent need to rebuild entire cities and industries. Half a trillion dollars from the US and EU would advance the WEF's Great Reset.

In his opening remarks at Davos Klaus Schwab said: "Our first thoughts are with the war in Ukraine. Russia's aggression on their [the Ukrainians'] country will be seen in future history books as the breakdown of the post-World War II and post-Cold War order. This is the reason why we speak about a turning-point in history. In Davos, our solidarity is foremost with the people suffering from the atrocities of this war."[52]

From the above it looks as if the competition between Russia/Gazprom and Ukraine/Royal Dutch Shell for the deposits of natural gas discovered in Ukrainian territory and under Ukraine's share of the Black Sea in 2012 has developed into a Russian "special military operation" and then a war of attrition between Russia and Ukraine with little possibility of a negotiated cease-fire and settlement, and the Great Reset's switch from oil and natural gas to green energy is already being implemented in the UN sanctions against Russian oil and natural gas. The UN that passed the sanctions is under Guterres, who is in partnership with Schwab and has been noticeably silent in trying to stop the fighting between Russia and Ukraine so as not to stall the Great Reset.

So Putin was *not* co-operating with his long-standing friend Schwab to deliver the Great Reset at the expense of Russian natural gas. At a political level he was provoked by events in Ukraine and sucked in to guard Russia's supplies of natural gas, but at a personal level he did not need much provoking as his following in the footsteps of Peter the Great (see p.98) makes clear. And while the UN under Guterres and the WEF under Schwab sought to bring in the Western Syndicate's New World Order by stripping Russia of its wealth (levelling Russia down), Russia was fighting in Ukraine to create a Russian New World Order that would eventually be based on the Soviet Union's pre-Gorbachev Eastern European Empire. And as we shall soon see, this looked bound to clash with the Western Syndicate's New World Order.

To sum up, Russia's invasion of Ukraine happened because Putin believed that:

- Ukraine's new gas deposits and the drilling of Royal Dutch Shell threatened to replace the export of Russia's natural gas;
- the Americans were behind the fall of Yanukovych and the ending of the association agreement with the EU;
- the Americans were creating biological weapons from viruses and biomaterials in biological laboratories in Ukraine that threatened Russia;
- most importantly, Ukraine had been Russian since Lenin's early days, and the Russian-speaking Donbas statelets of the People's Republics of Donetsk and Luhansk had to be Russianised and protected from Ukrainian attacks; and
- more importantly, Russia was seeking to take back its lost lands and return to Tsar Peter the Great's Empire and the pre-1991 Soviet states in Eastern Europe in a new Russian-shaped world order.

Putin, then, saw himself as a latter-day Peter the Great returning Russian lands to Russia, and Russia was seeking to revive a past period of greatness, a period of being a Great Power, by returning to Greater Russia and creating a coming Russian New World Order. But there was also a coming Western New World Order, and Biden had said that the Ukraine war was to determine whether the West or Russia would lead the coming New World Order.

What would the outcome be and had the Third World War already started? It is not impossible that our investigation of why Russia's invasion of Ukraine happened has already turned out to be an investigation into the causes of the Third World War.

3

What Happens Next:
A Third World War or a Further Fall of the West, a Coming New World Order

We saw on p.96 that on 24 February 2022 US State Department spokesman Ned Price said that both Russia and China "also [i.e. besides the West] want a World Order", but that theirs would be illiberal; and implied that the Russia-Ukraine war would determine who will rule the new "world order". We also saw on p.97 that on 21 March 2022 President Biden spoke of a coming "new world order": "There's going to be a new world order out there, and we've got to lead it. And we've got to unite the rest of the free world in doing it." Biden spoke as if the Third World War had already begun and implied that if we are not careful the fall of the West is about to happen. The Russian Foreign Minister warned Ukraine against provoking the Third World War (see p.119), and the new Head of the British Army spoke of fighting in Europe and winning what could only be the Third World War (see p.119).

Has the Third World War already started? It is possible to forecast the future by considering the alternatives that lie ahead for both sides on a step-by-step basis. We can number the 10 steps. Each step is slightly forward in time in relation to the previous step, and each step has consequences in relation to the next step.

Anticipating the future: looking ahead

1. *Russia winning.* In August 2022, Russia looked like winning in the east and south of Ukraine. The Ukrainians lacked weapons and ammunition, and Severodonetsk was fought for street-by-street, with the Russians' punishing fire-power pushing Ukrainian troops back. During the first 100 days of the Ukraine conflict Putin had funded his war machine with nearly $1 billion a day from fossil-fuel exports: the independent Centre for Research on Energy and Clean

111

Air (CREA) revealed that $98 billion (£80 billion) have reached the Kremlin in payments for oil and natural gas. The EU took 61 per cent of Russia's fossil-fuel exports during the war's first 100 days, worth about £50 billion. Outside the EU, China was top importer (£10.8 billion).

In early September 2022 the G7 capped the amount of Russian oil it would import to reduce Russian revenues that had been funding the war in Ukraine. Putin retaliated by getting Gazprom to shut down the Nord-Stream-1 natural-gas pipeline to Germany indefinitely. In so doing Putin immediately began to inflict immense, permanent damage on the Western way of life which could lead to enormous rises in the cost of household energy and vehicle fuel, poverty, civil disobedience, a new socialist government in and the break-up of the UK, nationalisations, price-and-incomes policies, wealth taxes and an economic and financial meltdown requiring a bail-out by the IMF. It threatened to increase European and UK expenditure to the level of the Great Depression of the 1930s.

2. *Russian withdrawal unlikely.* In this war of attrition with Russia slowly making gains, there could be a cease-fire, a peace settlement and a withdrawal of troops on both sides. Putin would want his gains of taken-back lands included in the peace agreement: in the Donbas region the People's Republics of Donetsk and Luhansk, and the eastern and southern parts of Ukraine including Mariupol and Severodonetsk, with control of all Ukraine's oil and natural gas.

A possible deal to end the war and bring about a Russian withdrawal would be for Russia, the US and NATO to recognise Ukraine's neutrality and allow Putin to keep Russia's ancestral access to the Black Sea via Crimea and its land bridge via Donetsk and Luhansk, to head off a possible Third World War and nuclear strike, but this would be resisted by Ukraine, which would want Russia to withdraw from every inch of Ukraine and Crimea, and by Russia, which would want the boundaries at the time of a cease-fire. An excellent deal would see Russia join the EU, or at least join a democratic multipolar New World Order that includes the four superpowers (the US, EU, Russia and China).

In August 2022 Putin ordered the Russian army to increase its forces by 137,000 soldiers, suggesting he was digging in for a long war.

At the St Petersburg International Economic Forum on 17 June 2022 Putin again compared himself to Peter the Great and asserted that Russia has the right to "take back" any territory it once controlled. It was now clear that he wants Russia to be a great power, and that without Ukraine Russia cannot be that great power. Moreover, if the Ukrainians' democratic experiment is allowed to work, Putin fears that Russians will want to do the same, and to keep Russia potentially great and Putin's imperial dream alive, Ukraine must be reduced to rubble and later rebuilt – as happened to the Chechnyan capital Grozny. As Calgacus, the chieftain of the Caledonian Confederacy who fought the Roman army of Julius Caesar, said according to Tacitus: "They make a desert and call it 'peace'." Putin's flattening of Chechnya, Syria and now eastern Ukraine into rubble recalls the Roman approach.

At the Economic Forum Russian officials displayed a map showing a plan for administering the whole of Ukraine over a three-to-five-year period. The conquests will not stop at Donetsk and Luhansk, and there can be no cease-fire with the giving-up of lands Russia controls as Putin wants *all* Ukraine, and Ukraine will not agree to give up an inch. Putin, urged on by his friend the banker Yury Kovalchuk, who spent evenings with him when he was isolating from Covid in 2020 talking about Ukraine's perfidy, and also by his new aggressive secretary to Russia's security council Nikolai Patrushev, in effect Putin's national security adviser, now saw Russia as being at war with the West and was persuaded that wars must be fought without limits or mercy.

Putin has modelled himself on Ivan Ilyin, the fascist philosopher who became his guide: a supporter of the far right who became a counter-revolutionary against the Bolsheviks.[1] In his first address to the Russian parliament as president in 2012 Putin saw himself as the medieval warlord of Kyiv Russians called Vladimir (a Russianisation of Volodymyr or Valdemar) who converted to Christianity in 988 and linked the lands of Russia, Belarus and Ukraine. It is easy to imagine how galling it must have been for Putin that the new warlord of Kyiv was not Vladimir (his own name) but Volodymyr (Zelensky), who wanted Ukraine to join the EU and so was "a fascist" – in the sense of a follower of Germany, which was Fascist during the war, not in the sense of following the fascist philosopher Ilyin.[2]

Since, as a latter-day Peter the Great, Putin was going for the conquest of all Ukraine, there was a case for believing that only the defeat of Putin and withdrawal of Russian troops could lead to a sustainable peace. Some Western commentators believed that Putin's invasion would accelerate Russia's decline as it had completely alienated all Ukrainians, who would have nothing to do with Russia and would fight what had in effect become a guerrilla war without the weapons they wanted and needed having arrived, and hope they would hold out. But it looked more likely that Russia would succeed in taking the whole of Ukraine, especially when it was announced that Russia would supply its navy in the Black Sea with Zircon hypersonic missiles that travel nine times faster than the speed of sound and cannot be intercepted – unless Putin stopped the Russian progress and withdrew all his troops to Russia in return for recognition that the cease-fire line is a new Russia-Ukraine border without Western sanctions against Russia remaining in place until the full withdrawal of Russian forces from Ukraine, which was extremely unlikely.

3. *Western support for peace on Putin's terms unlikely.* But the West (the US, EU, the UK and NATO) were unlikely to support a peace agreement on Putin's terms. The feeling was abroad that Putin should not profit from his "special military operation". The Western countries and NATO forces would therefore urge Ukraine not to give in and would continue to arm Ukraine, even though the Russians destroyed more and more of Ukraine. The likelihood was that the war would continue.

NATO had no choice but to support Kyiv as the West's future security depended on holding the line in Ukraine. Western support for Ukraine had appeared to be flagging, but in preparation for its Madrid conference in June 2022 NATO expanded. Sweden and Finland both joined, and there was now a new Iron Curtain drawn by the West along its border with Russia, Belarus and Ukraine, from

Estonia to Latvia, Lithuania, Poland, Slovakia, Hungary, Romania and Bulgaria, in each of which Allied troops were deployed with 24/7 air patrol and surveillance. Two extra squadrons of US F-35 fighters were to be deployed at RAF Lakenheath in Suffolk, UK. At its Madrid meeting NATO increased its troops by 300,000 and the UK pledged another £1 billion towards the fighting in Ukraine. There was now a 300,000-strong high-readiness force with ships and aircraft defending NATO's east, a sevenfold increase from 40,000, and NATO had a new strategy following the biggest overhaul of collective defence and deterrence since the end of the Cold War, reversing the "peace dividend" (through reducing the size of armies) from 1991.

The Prime Minister of Estonia (another territory Russia wants to take back), Kaja Kallas, wrote in an article,[3] "Russia's war in Ukraine has fundamentally changed the security environment in Europe." She wrote that the Kremlin, including Putin, have made it clear that "their aim is to wipe Ukraine off the world map" and: "We must do all we can to help push back the Russian invasion and end massive war crimes at our doorstep. Otherwise, worse will follow." She was thinking that Estonia might be next.

Latvia's Foreign Minister was reported on the same day as calling for the West to support Ukraine "for as long as it takes" on a "war footing".[4]

This feeling about Russia is similar to the feeling about Germany in the 1930s, when Hitler took back first the Rhineland (1936); then Austria (1938); then the Sudetenland (1938); then Czechoslovakia (1938); and finally Poland (1939). Putin attacked Chechnya (2005); Georgia, the land where the phoenix is said to have originated (2008), and now occupies 20 per cent of it in South Ossetia and Abkhazia; then Crimea (2014); now parts of Ukraine have been annexed, starting with Donetsk and Luhansk, and continuing with Kherson and Zaporizhzhia (2022). Next perhaps Estonia, which would involve a collision with NATO.

Kissinger has spoken of Russia as a "declining" country (see p.122). Russia does not have enough troops to launch a big push in Ukraine without declaring a full-scale war and mobilising reserves.

The Ukrainians have not the weapons to win on the battlefield because of the sheer size of Russia's army and the Western tactic of backing Ukraine seems doomed to fail. With autumn approaching and bad weather hindering air power and swollen rivers, there is the prospect of a stalemate.

So either the war in Ukraine is stopped by a cease-fire, talks and a Russian withdrawal, as Kissinger would like to see (see p.122), and perhaps Putin would retire to his rest-house-cum-sanatorium and be replaced. Or Russia continues fighting until it has taken back its former lands, so long as Putin is well enough to lead Russia and is not deposed. In which case the West needs to defeat Russia, as the Estonian Prime Minister said. If it doesn't, the war of taking back past lands threatens to become a war of attrition with the ever-present fear of Russia's RS-28 hypersonic intercontinental ballistic missiles an ever-increasing threat to the West, the very dangerous Cold War 2 that Kissinger drew attention to. And it can bring about a further fall, and levelling-down of the West, and threatens to spread into the Third World War.

There were signs in June 2022 that the West was escalating its support for Ukraine. The leaders of Germany, France and Italy went to Kyiv and met Zelensky to speed up Ukraine's joining of the EU in defiance of Putin. The three leaders seemed to have urged Zelensky to reach a settlement with Russia. Scholz of Germany announced that Zelensky was to take part in the next G7 meeting. The next day the President of the EU Commission, Ursula von der Leyen, proposed that Ukraine should become a candidate for EU membership, but there were still conditions to be satisfied. The next day Johnson, the UK's prime minister, visited Ukraine and promised to supply missiles that would expel Russians from Ukraine, further making the UK a possible future Russian target. A few days later the EU accepted Ukraine and Moldova as candidates for the EU and granted them candidate status.

Also, Ukrainians were taking the war inside Russia, and the supply of Russia's natural gas was now a Ukrainian target. There were two fires at the Transneft-Druzhba oil depot in Bryansk on 25 April 2022 after suspected Ukrainian missile strikes; the Druzhba pipeline is one of the main routes by which Russian oil reaches Europe. Ukrainian forces were thought to be operating behind Russian lines to cause these fires and hamper Russia's funding of the war from receipts from oil and natural gas. On 16 June Gazprom reported that Russia's largest gas field was ablaze after a pipe burst around 2.30am at the Urengoyskoye gas field in the Yamalo-Nenets region of Siberia, sending huge flames into the night sky. Urengoyskoye is the world's largest gas deposit and supplies Europe via the Yamal–Europe pipeline, and there were immediate fears of supply disruptions and rising prices for gas in Europe. Ukrainian sabotage was suspected.[5] And there have been attacks on Crimea.

4. *Putin can win by taking back once-Russian lands.* In the war of attrition, Putin can widen the war to taking back Transnistria and perhaps part of Moldova, and to taking back Abkhazia and South Ossetia on the border of Georgia. Worryingly Medvedev has posted to his 2.2 million followers that Georgia "didn't exist as a state" before joining Russia in the 1800s, and that Kazakhstan is an "artificial state". At this point the war will be spreading. Russia's long-term plan to expand its territories included the Arctic. The think tank Civitas warned in a report that Russia had reopened 50 Soviet-era military posts, airbases and radar stations in the Arctic during the last decade and was moving its nuclear deterrent to the Arctic region to make the Arctic the "battleground of the future". If the Western countries and NATO forces concede these territories, then Russia gains, just as it did when the West and NATO in effect conceded Crimea. This will mark a further stage in the West's decline and levelling-down. If Putin plans to take back Estonia (a member of NATO), whose population is only 1.3 million, there is likely to be NATO-led resistance, and if Putin were to enter Poland (a member of NATO), which has a population of 37.7 million, there would definitely be NATO-led resistance and the Third World War would be underway just as the Second World War was declared immediately following Hitler's invasion of Poland.

What Russia could do is, frankly, terrifying. Russia has annexed the portions of Ukraine under Russian control, including the two rebel "People's Republics" in the Donbas region, Donetsk and Luhansk, and it could also swallow Abkhazia and South Ossetia in Georgia, and Belarus (changing the existing "Union State of Russia and Belarus" into a form of words suggesting Belarus was an integral part of Greater Russia). Putin could then compare himself to Ivan the Great (or Terrible), who defeated the Tatars and "gathered the Russian lands" at the end of the 15th century, three centuries before Peter the Great. But it must be remembered that Russia is a declining country and can only pay for a taking-back of its territories, a gathering of its former lands, by seizing assets in the countries it invades. (There was news in June 2022 that Ukrainian stores of grain were being pillaged and loaded onto Russian ships for sale to other countries.)

As we have seen (on p.115), Hitler invaded the Rhineland, Austria, the Sudetenland and Czechoslovakia before he invaded Poland and began the Second World War. Putin has invaded Chechnya, Georgia, Crimea, Ukraine and has annexed Donetsk and Luhansk and other Ukrainian territories such as lands around Kherson and Zaporizhzhia, and if his health permits could continue with Abkhazia and South Ossetia, Transnistria and Moldova, Belarus, Estonia and Poland. At what point would the West say "Enough" and declare a Third World War? NATO is primed to defend Estonia and Poland.

5. *The Third World War imminent.* The more the Western countries and NATO fight and resist Putin's spreading of the war, the more is the likelihood that a Third World War is breaking out: a Third World War between on one side the democratic West and NATO and on the other side the autocratic and authoritarian regimes of both Russia and China. All three have hypersonic nuclear weapons, and this would be the most dangerous crisis since the Second World War.

On 18 June 2022 Putin made a speech at the St Petersburg International Economic Forum. Looking sweaty and bloated from his steroids a week after being taken ill with "weakness and dizziness" after getting up from his desk following a 90-minute virtual session with his military chiefs, which required urgent medical assistance, Putin warned the West that he would use nuclear weapons if he was threatened. He said that while he was not threatening the world with nuclear weapons, he was ready to use them to protect Russia: "We are not threatening. But everyone needs to know we have [the nuclear bomb] and we will use it if necessary to protect our sovereignty." He declared the end of "the era of the unipolar world" led by the US, the sole superpower after winning the Cold War, and announced "a multipolar world".

Also on 18 June 2022 Putin shared a platform at the St Petersburg International Economic Forum's plenary session in St Petersburg with the leader of Kazakhstan, Kassym-Jomart Tokayev, who refused to recognise the Donetsk and Luhansk People's Republics as independent states. Putin was furious and felt humiliated. The Chechen leader warned Kazakhstan it had to stand with Russia. General SVR channel claimed that Putin had not ruled out a major mobilisation of half a million men in five regions of western Russia close to Ukraine (Bryansk, Kursk, Belgorod, Voronezh and Rostov). There were also Ukrainian reports that Putin was pressuring the dictator of Belarus, Aleksandr Lukashenko, into opening a second front by invading the Volyn, Rivne and Kyiv regions of Ukraine.

NATO Secretary-General Jens Stoltenberg said the conflict in Ukraine could last for years and urged Western governments to send state-of-the-art weaponry to Ukrainian troops, Germany's *Bild am Sonntag* newspaper reported.

The UK had decided by mid-June 2022 that there would be a long war. The new Army Commander, General Sir Patrick Sanders, wrote to all 73,000 soldiers saying they must get ready to fight the Russians and win a potential Third World War: "We are the generation that must prepare the Army to fight in Europe once again." The Army had to "deter Russian aggression with the threat of force".

On 26 April 2022 the Russian Foreign Minister, Sergei Lavrov, claimed that NATO was "in essence" engaged in a proxy war with Russia by supplying Kyiv with weaponry, and that there was a "real" danger of his country's invasion of Ukraine escalating into World War Three. Lavrov warned Ukraine against provoking the Third World War, and said the threat of a nuclear conflict "should not be underestimated".[6]

When in June 2022 Lithuania, a NATO state, blocked EU-sanctioned goods (coal, steel, metals, construction materials and advanced technology) from reaching Kaliningrad, Russia's exclave, retired Russian General Evgeny Buzhinsky urged Putin to send nuclear weapons to Kaliningrad. A direct Russian attack on Lithuania would be seen as an act of war against NATO and could start a Third World War. Buzhinsky threatened that Britain will "physically cease to exist" if the stand-off in Lithuania triggered a nuclear Third World War. Taking issue with Sanders' call to British troops to prepare to fight and beat Russian forces in what could only be a Third World War, Buzhinsky said, "He doesn't understand that as a result of a Third World War Britain will physically cease to exist. The island will vanish, so I've no idea where he or his descendants will live." In mid-July Lithuania allowed Russian goods to cross its territory on their way to Russia's Kaliningrad exclave.

The UK's Prime Minister Boris Johnson urged Western leaders to "steel" themselves for a long war in Ukraine or risk "the greatest victory for aggression in Europe since the Second World War". This would mean constant funding of the Ukrainian state to enable it to pay wages, run schools, deliver aid and begin reconstruction (estimated in June 2022 at more than $100 billion by the Kyiv School of Economics, see p.108 for Zelensky's estimate of $500 billion). It would mean technical support and supply of weapons, equipment and ammunition from the British people still reeling from the 4.5-per-cent drop in GDP following Brexit (an annual loss which the Office of Budget Responsibility has estimated at £80 billion), the pandemic, the £100-billion-a-year increase in raised interest rates to service the debt of more than £2 trillion, and the cost-of-living crisis with inflation at 11 per cent and the return of 1970s-style strikes: a promise that might have to be withdrawn. For could the UK Government really further borrow to pay all the Ukrainian State salaries when it could not pay its own State salaries and NHS bills? Johnson said Putin's determination to "take back" any territory ever inhabited by "Slavs" would permit the conquest of vast expanses of Europe, including territories of NATO allies. Meanwhile all dictators would be emboldened to invade their neighbours.

6. *Further Western fall possible.* If Russia takes back Estonia (a member of NATO) and/or advances into Poland (a member of NATO) without any or much resistance on the part of the West, or if there is a peace settlement that allows Russia to keep its taken-back lands, then the West will have undergone a further fall. This would be a worse situation than the Western withdrawal from Afghanistan in bringing public visibility to, and focus on, Western impotence and decline.

7. *Russian New World Order possible.* When Russia has finished its taking-back, which might be during the course of the Third World War, if Russia wins, meaning if the West is defeated or reaches a peace agreement that allows Russia to retain its taken-back lands, then there will be a Russian New World Order in conjunction with China, an autocratic and authoritarian New World Order that will involve the Syndicate. The West will be a subordinate sharer in this New World Order, whose terms will be dictated by the East, with China getting stronger and dominating the New World Order.

8. *Western Syndicate New World Order possible.* If Russia is defeated, and justifies Kissinger's view it is a declining power, then there will be a democratic Western New World Order that will involve the Syndicate, with Russia as a subordinate sharer in the New World Order and China as a sullen partner that will be getting stronger and pushing to dominate the New World Order. It will not be long before the West and China confront each other.

9. *A clash between two Syndicate-led New World Orders.* The Russian-Ukrainian war was therefore a clash between two Syndicate-led spheres of influence and New World Orders, the Russian and the Western, that were rising phoenix-like from the ashes of (in Schwab's words in 2022) "the breakdown of the post-World-War-II and post-Cold-War order". The world order of post-1945 and post-1991 had come to an end, and a New World Order was being created in the fighting in Ukraine, which had replaced the coronavirus pandemic as a means of controlling Western and Eastern populations in the run-in to this New World Order. And while this was happening, China, whose Belt-and-Road Initiative was now in 140 countries

and already creating a new Chinese world order, was watching, supporting Russia against the West, temporarily paralysed by its internal pandemic lockdowns, but nevertheless waiting ominously to advance its own Chinese New World Order.

In an interview with Niall Ferguson on 12 June 2022,[7] the 99-year-old Henry Kissinger said that Putin was "head of a declining country" and "he's lost his sense of proportion in this crisis". He said, "The question will now be how to end that war. At its end a place has to be found for Ukraine and a place has to be found for Russia – if we don't want Russia to become an outpost of China in Europe."

Kissinger added, "Two countries with the capacity to dominate the world" – the US and China – "are facing each other as the ultimate contestants. They are governed by incompatible domestic systems. And this is occurring when technology means that a war would set back civilisation, if not destroy it." In other words, Cold War 2 is even more dangerous than Cold War 1, because the technologies of destruction are even more terrifying, especially with the advent of artificial intelligence.

As President Biden said (see p.109), the war in Ukraine was a war between Russia and the West to decide who will lead the New World Order. America wants to lead the West and the New World Order. But so does Putin, following in the footsteps of Peter the Great (see pp.98–99, 108). If Putin was deliberately provoked by the Great Reset (see pp.105–108), that provocation was a miscalculation as it allowed Putin to go into Ukraine and do in the south what Peter the Great had done in the north before founding St Petersburg: (as he saw it) take back Russian lands after being in power for 23 years.

The crucial question was, had Putin accelerated Russia's decline or would he achieve a Greater Russia that would lead a New World Order?

We have seen (on pp.105–108, 121) that the World Economic Forum was expressing the West's condemnation of Russia's invasion of Ukraine, and that Schwab spoke of "the breakdown of the post-World-War-II and post-Cold-War order". It was time for there to be a New World Order, and we have seen that the West was seeking to create its own New World Order: a Western sphere of influence primed to dominate the world in alliance with its supporters within the Syndicate. We have also seen that Russia was re-creating its own sphere of influence through the invasion of Ukraine that might also be primed to dominate the world in alliance with its supporters ('Rockefellers') within the Syndicate. China, too, had its sphere of influence. The world had split into three spheres of influence, two of which were at proxy-war.

10. *Syndicate's 'Triple-Code' New World Order possible.* Whatever the outcome, whichever side emerges from the war in Ukraine as the winner, the Syndicate will be crucial in shaping the New World Order that will include the West, Russia and China as a kind of triangular 'Triple Code'. There will be space between all three, the West, Russia and China, but they will be intricately bound together. In the Triple Code there is always a round circle at the top (see illustration below). In the same way, whatever the outcome of the conflict in Ukraine, in the Triple Code one of the three nation-states – the US, Russia and China – will dominate by being on top, above the two below.

Lapel badge showing the Triple Code (see p.48).

It looked as if a Western Syndicate phoenix was rising from the ashes of the Western financial system it will destroy, from the ashes of the world order since the Second World War and the end of the Cold War, and that a Russian phoenix was rising from the ashes of its post-Second-World-War and Cold-War order, which will include much of Ukraine and be authoritarian; and that a Chinese phoenix was rising from the ashes of the Communist Cold War based on the Belt-and-Road Initiative in 140 countries, and will be expansionist in the Pacific area. It looked as if we were living in the time of the breaking-down of a world order that had lasted from 1945 until 2022 – until the invasion of Ukraine.

11. *Use of nuclear weapons possible.* The process of a Syndicate New World Order can be speeded up by the use of nuclear weapons. By June 2022 it was clear that Russia was reviving a power it had under the Soviet Union, and that there could be a Third World War if the West supplied lethal weapons to Ukraine that began to tilt the nature of the proxy war in Ukraine in the West's favour. The Western powers and NATO were careful not to supply missiles that could reach far into Russia, and provoke Russia into using nuclear weapons: its RS-28 hypersonic interconnected ballistic missiles, one of which could destroy an area the size of the UK or France.

But Deagel.com forecast reductions in the populations of the US, the UK and EU by 2025 (see p.101), and in 2024 if the war of attrition was continuing and spreading Russia could deliver nuclear strikes with its hypersonic ballistic missiles that would keep the population below 8 billion in accordance with the Syndicate's planning – and take a short cut to a Russian New World Order with the Syndicate's involvement, and further levelling-down of the West.

However we look at the future, the Syndicate are behind the eventual Triple Code with one of the US, Russia and China on top of the other two, within a Syndicate New World Order.

It is now time to look at each sphere of influence and conflicting New World Order in greater detail, to see if we can find a way forward. This means examining all the evidence and, as in a jigsaw puzzle, interlocking as many pieces as possible to give a picture of what the future holds.

1. Possible Western New World Order

The Western New World Order has been prepared for some time.

Nelson Rockefeller's New World Order

As I showed in *The Syndicate* and in *The Fall of the West*[8] the term 'New World Order' was first used in the modern media by New York Governor Nelson Rockefeller in 1962 when he called for world federalism in his book *The Future of Federalism* (1962), claiming that a "new world order" was needed as the old order was crumbling. "There will evolve the bases for a federal structure of the free world." Then Nelson Rockefeller was quoted in *AP* (26 July 1968) as saying that "as President he would work towards international creation of a 'new world order'", and in 1990 Bush Sr said that "a New World Order can emerge" that could "shape the future for generations to come".

From the outset the Western concept of a New World Order was 'Rockefellerite'.

Pax Americana

The idea of a federal Western New World Order has come to suggest a US hegemony's *Pax Americana*, with America imposing peace and order while fighting in Vietnam (which went wrong when the US had to evacuate), Afghanistan and Iraq. However, the Western New World Order suffered a reverse in Syria, where an alliance between Assad and Russia won but flattened much of Syria, causing 13.2 million Syrians to be displaced, and at least 6.7 million to leave the country as refugees by the end of 2019; and in Afghanistan, where the West withdrew and allowed the Taliban to take over and medievalise the country Westerners had spent so much time and investment and so many lives in shoring up.

The Western response in Ukraine was sluggish, and Ukraine only received a handful of multiple-launch rocket systems instead of the 300 Zelensky said he needed, allowing Russia to fire 50,000 shells a day and cause the Ukrainians to fall back with a casualty rate of up to 800 a day. America and the rest of the West forecast a Russian defeat but did little to stop Putin, and China took note that America's lack of resolve in Afghanistan and Ukraine might allow a Chinese invasion of Taiwan to succeed.

There were signs that at the end of August 2022 America had grown weary of the war in Ukraine, its focus having switched to a coming American economic slump, the rising threat of a conflict with China, unease at Ukrainian corruption, and the rising cost of energy in Europe.

The Great Reset added to the Western New World Order

The Western New World Order has been reinforced by the World Economic Forum's economic plans for the West. In fact, the World Economic Forum's 'Great Reset' has rebranded Rockefellers' New World Order. Central to the 'Great Reset' is technocracy, and the book by Zbigniew Brzezinski, *Between Two Ages: America's Role in the Technetronic Era* (1970), which examined the impact of the ongoing technological revolution (the internet, mobile phones) on the institutions and political values of the US and other industrial nations. Technocracy is a form of government in which decision-makers are selected for their technical knowledge, which in turn becomes technological surveillance to maintain public order and uses technology to extend the length of human life and resist illness and disease in a mass transformation of the human condition.

The Great Reset has been prepared for by the Rockefeller Foundation's work on a coming pandemic, food shortages and a collapsing economy. In 2010 the Rockefeller Foundation published a report titled *Scenario for the Future of Technology and International Development*, which included a "Lock Step" scenario, a co-ordinated global response to a lethal pandemic which now seems to have been a dress rehearsal for the similar Covid pandemic. Lock Step had restrictions on citizens, compulsory mask-wearing and body-temperature checks.[9] This was followed by 'Event 201', which was mounted by the Johns Hopkins Center for Health Security in partnership with the World Economic Forum and the Bill and Melinda Gates Foundation (and the CIA), and was funded by Bill Gates. It anticipates the Covid Plan.[10] In April 2020 the Rockefeller Foundation released its *National Covid-19 Testing Action Plan*, which set out a program of travel restrictions, surveillance and social control that limited liberty and freedom of choice. Its tracking system was similar to what was later used in China.

Then in July 2020 the Rockefeller Foundation published *Reset the Table: Meeting the Moment to Transform the US Food System*, which dealt with famine and food shortages, and seizing control of the food supply chain and running it fairly and to protect the environment. This was part of the World Economic Forum's 'The Great Reset', which was officially announced by Schwab, the founder of the World Economic Forum, and Prince Charles on 3 June 2020, and in the foreword of *Reset the Table* the Rockefeller Foundation's President Dr Rajav Shah called for a playbook to cover the food system, wages and housing, all of which would need to be (intentionally) revised during the Great Reset. It is not known if Prince Charles realised the Great Reset's implications regarding intentional loss of ownership (see p.105) following Schwab's technocratic revolution when he co-announced the Great Reset in 2020.

The Great Reset is not restoring society to the pre-Covid days, as Schwab believes that cannot happen. It is producing a new society in which humans are merged with machines, and physical and biological systems are merged with digital systems: the Fourth Industrial Revolution, a fusion of artificial intelligence (AI), robotics, the Internet of Things (IoT), 3D printing, genetic engineering, quantum computing, cyber-physical systems (CPS), cloud computing, cognitive computing and other technologies. This will affect the way we live, work and relate to each other, and there may be more working from home using new technology.

More companies may employ specialist contractors or remote workers. A downside will be the effects of the Fourth Industrial Revolution on climate change: rapid development of technologies can be expected to lead to massive industrialisation, increased urbanisation, deforestation, rapid population growth and water scarcity.

In the world of the Great Reset, overpopulation will be controlled by the metaverse, in which there will be virtual children. There will be selective breeding of physical bodies in artificial wombs.

To technocracy humans are natural resources. Parents will interact with these virtual children wearing high-tech gloves that will have tactile sensations that replicate physical sensations – another way the distinction between men and machines can be blurred. The unelected few will run the world through algorithms and AI, and humankind will be enslaved. Humans will be connected to the cloud and able to access the internet through their brains. Beliefs will be downloaded from the cloud, and also instructions as to what servile humans are to do. There will be no free will, humans will accept orders, and there will be carbon footprint trackers, which have already been developed by the Chinese Alibaba Group, plans for the use of which were announced at the World Economic Forum's 2022 Davos meeting. People will live in automated 'smart cities', their food will include laboratory-created meat ("fake meat") in place of real meat. Food will include bugs, crickets, beetles and insects; weeds; and reclaimed sewage.

I should point out that the First Industrial Revolution can be dated to 1760–1820 (the power loom in 1765, transition from creating goods by hand to using machines, proto-industrialisation and the harnessing of steam for mechanical production from 1784); the Second Industrial Revolution to 1871–1914 (rail, telegraph wires, electrical power, telephone); and the Third Industrial Revolution to the years following 1969 (nuclear energy, electronics, telecommunications and computers). The Fourth Industrial Revolution can be dated from 2015 to the present (the blurring of borders between the physical, biological and digital worlds, fusion of technologies, automation, robots and data exchange).

The World Economic Forum was born from a CIA-funded Harvard program headed by Henry Kissinger and supported by J.K. Galbraith and Herman Kahn, who all had links to the Council of Foreign Relations and the Round Table Movement. Kissinger, a professor at Harvard in Cambridge, Massachusetts, ran an International Seminar that was attended by Klaus Schwab. On 16 April 1967 it was reported that Harvard programs had been receiving funding from the CIA, including $135,000 for Kissinger's International Seminar, which Kissinger denied being aware of. The evidence is that Schwab was recruited by Kissinger to his circle of 'Round Table' imperialists via a CIA-funded program at Harvard.

This Seminar introduced Schwab to the US policy-makers who would help him create the most powerful European public policy institution, the World Economic Forum. In 1980 Kissinger, having since run American foreign policy, made the opening address at the World Economic Forum's 1980 conference, and in his speech said, "For the first time in history, foreign policy is truly global."

Central to the Great Reset is digitalising money. 'Rothschilds', who own or control most of the world's central banks, will use central bank digital currency (CBDC) in their central-bank systems, and smart contracts will allow banks to control what people spend their money on and to control human lives.

The World Bank and global networks are already promoting digital ID in the Global South, biometric digital systems involving thumbprints which allow surveillance and are dangerous for human rights. Concerns have been set out in *Paving a Digital Road to Hell? A Primer on the Role of the World Bank and Global Networks in Promoting Digital ID*, issued by the Center for Human Rights and Global Justice at New York University School of Law. The concerns grew out of the 2019 Special Rapporteur's Report to the UN General Assembly on digital welfare states. The World Bank's ID4D (Identification for Development) has been legally funded by the Bill and Melinda Gates Foundation ($27 million to date) and the whole concept is linked to the digitalising of money by the Great Reset.

Schwab collaborated with Bill Gates by hosting the Event 201 conference in October 2019 which modelled a fictional coronavirus pandemic. (See p.126.) In July 2020 Schwab brought out *Covid-19: The Great Reset*, co-authored with Thierry Malleret, to show what the post-pandemic might, or perhaps should, look like. The title associates Covid with the Great Reset, the Reset being a re-setting of the world after Covid which makes it clear that the world after the reset would be different: "The pandemic will accelerate innovation even more, catalysing technological changes already under way."

Overtly the World Economic Forum is against the Russian invasion: it has an exhibition on Russian war crimes in Ukraine in the foyer of the 'Russian House' at Davos, as we have seen (p.106), and Zelensky addressed the World Economic Forum's meeting in

Davos on 23 May 2022. The St Petersburg International Economic Forum is Russia's equivalent to the World Economic Forum, and is different. It had Putin as a speaker on 18 June 2022, and he and Medvedev have addressed the International Economic Forum in St Petersburg five times since 2007. During the 2017 meeting of the St Petersburg International Economic Forum, which aims to rival the World Economic Forum and is regarded as being comparable to it, the Russian Roscongrass Foundation and the World Economic Forum signed a memorandum of co-operation, and the Roscongrass Foundation has hosted the 'Russian House' at Davos since 2018. On 27 November 2019 Putin met Schwab in St Petersburg.

The Great Reset has to be fulfilled by 2030, and so needs to be got on with now. We have already found (see p.107) that the Russian-Ukraine war was not a World Economic Forum strategy to accelerate the Great Reset by curtailing the world's oil and gas, compelling the world to promote green energy, and that Schwab, who is in partnership with Guterres to deliver the 17 sustainable goals economically, was not in a hidden partnership with Putin in which Putin took back tracts of Russia's past lands in eastern Ukraine and got the Great Reset going. We have found there is no evidence of such collusion, only speculation.

Putin has challenged the Western New World Order by invading Ukraine

In fact, Russia's invasion of Ukraine has had the effect of challenging the US's Western New World Order, by inviting it to confront Russia and be diminished if it does not do so for fear of starting a Third World War. The West's subsequent blocking of Russia's oil and gas entering the EU has forced green alternatives onto the EU countries most affected, such as Germany, when they are not yet ready to make a wholesale change to green. The Syndicate support the Great Reset, and it is possible that Putin has lured the West into cutting off Russian oil and gas for a while to defeat the West and the Syndicate, sow confusion in the Western economy, divide the West on oil and gas and demonstrate the West's impotence. Putin seems to have been seeking to demonstrate that the Western New World Order based on the Great Reset is half-baked and incapable of stopping Russia's agenda to take back once-Russian lands. Putin seems to have provoked the West into demonstrating its weakness in failing to support Ukraine in its battle with Russia, and into demonstrating the weakness of the Western New World Order. Besides taking back lands, Putin seems to have invaded Ukraine to challenge the American New World Order and its Great Reset, to bring it out into the open and expose its emptiness when it stops short of invading Ukraine for fear of starting a Third World War.

The US's Western New World Order has been admitted to by the US State Department spokesman Ned Price when he said that both Russia and China want an illiberal New World Order (see p.96), and implied that out of Ukraine America would be seeking to bring in a liberal New World Order. The US has had a policy of extending NATO, pushing it eastwards to help Ukraine and extending NATO's border to include the newly-joined NATO countries Sweden and Finland so an Iron Curtain now separates Russia from Western and Eastern Europe.

The Western New World Order is essentially the rules-based international order the UN has defended since 1945, which rests on an alliance between the US, the EU and the NATO states. It is complicit in what happened to Ukraine by intervening and causing the Maidan-Square revolution and so far as the evidence suggests by introducing up to 30 biological laboratories into Ukraine. The Western alliance that includes the EU extends to Israel.

The Western New World Order (the US, the Syndicate and the EU and their allies) has incorporated the World Economic Forum, and its method of governing will be technocratic and digital, and will use artificial intelligence, as we have just seen. It will control humans by regarding them as machines, while still standing for freedom, democracy, human rights and rule of law – and the rules-based international order which has failed to prevent a creeping autocracy and authoritarianism from taking over many nation-states, led by admirers of the Russian and Chinese leaderships.

Only 1 billion of the 7.96 billion world population in mid-2022 live in the West. With its allies the West comprises the EU, the UK, Norway, Iceland, Switzerland, the United States, Canada, Australia and New Zealand. The Western New World Order looks like a golden phoenix rising from the ashes of decolonisation and the loss of Western influence since 1991, but now the world is multipolar nearly 7 billion of the world population do not want to be ruled by what they regard as a Western regional grouping. And they may not be persuaded to follow the technocratic AI life-style the Western New World Order is now offering.

2. Possible Russian New World Order

In 19th-century Russia there were Russian Westernisers who looked to Europe and the West, like Turgenev, and Slavophiles who regarded Russia as being non-Western and separate, with its own destiny, like Dostoevsky. During the Cold War Russia was opposed to the West. From 1985 Gorbachev embraced Western values and openness (*glasnost*), a more open consultative government and wider dissemination of information. Putin has returned to opposing the West, regarding it as pressing on Russia's borders and trying to intervene.

On 19 July 2022 Putin visited Iran and with Iran's leaders (President Raisi and the Supreme Leader Ayatollah Khamenei) and President Erdogan of Turkey ostensibly discussed Syria but in fact formed an anti-Western and anti-democratic alliance. Russia signed a deal with Iran to develop the Iranian gas and oil industry worth $33 billion, and Iran applied to join the BRICS trading group of Brazil, Russia, India, China and South Africa. Behind Russia, Iran and Turkey is China, which was developing the world's largest navy in terms of its number of ships and wanted access to cheap Russian and Iranian oil and gas and Russian grain. The alliance of Russia-Turkey-Iran-probably Syria-Ukraine-China would stretch from Eastern Europe across Eurasia to the South China Sea, with Russia at its centre, a Russian New World Order. Putin has led the way in creating this new anti-Western alliance that can potentially dominate the world by invading Ukraine.

The presence of Turkey's President along with Putin in Iran had one good result on 22 July 2022 when a deal brokered by the UN and Turkey was signed by both Ukraine's infrastructure minister and Russia's defence minister in Istanbul. The signing ceremony was attended by President Erdogan and Guterres, the UN Secretary-General, and the deal allowed the export of millions of tonnes of grain from blockaded Black-Sea ports and averted a catastrophic global food crisis. It enabled the shipping of grain from Ukraine to resume and saved the poorest in African and Middle-Eastern countries dependent on Ukraine's grain from long-term malnutrition, hunger and famine. The Turkish President's presence in Iran with Putin may have steered the unprecedented deal between Russia and Ukraine, two warring countries, to a successful outcome, and it presented Putin in a responsible, humanitarian statesman-like light.

However, Putin does not make deals that do not benefit him, and the legitimising of this deal can ease Russia's trade in shipping stolen grain from Ukraine and may ease Western sanctions. The monitoring of the shipping from a co-ordination centre in Istanbul by UN staff and military officials from Russia, Ukraine and Turkey can be (as in the past) a base from which Russians can spy on troop movements and supply lines within Ukraine. A Russian missile strike on Odesa within 24 hours of the signing seemed to make clear that the deal to ship grain from Odesa is within a continuation of the war in Odesa, contrary to what the UN thought – and cast doubt on the viability of the deal.

Russia has challenged the Western rules-based international order which Putin saw as NATO threatening Russia's borders. Putin has begun to try to revert to Greater Russia with some of the lands that were Russian during the Soviet Union, and has dreamt of a "common economic space" that extends from the Atlantic to the Pacific, from Lisbon to Vladivostok in the Arctic Circle, as Putin said in 2010. The Russian Federation is enormous, it is twice as wide as the US or China, but it only had a population of around 146 million in 2022 against 289 million in 1991. If it were to reach Lisbon and add the Balkans and take over Belarus as well as Ukraine, a Russian New World Order would include some of Eastern and Western Europe and much of Eurasia. And Putin has been looking towards Eurasia.

Russia now looks towards Eurasia. On 27 February 2012, in an article in *Moskovskie Novosti* (based on his article in a German newspaper in 2010, see p.98), Putin proposed a "Eurasian Union" as an alternative

The map shown on p.97, but with a new eastern significance: Putin's "common economic space" with a new focus on Eurasia.

to the European Union, the EU. In the long run, Putin explained in the article, Eurasia would overwhelm the EU in a larger "Union of Europe", a "space" ("common economic space") between the Atlantic and the Pacific, from "Lisbon to Vladivostok" (see pp.98, 133). Not to join Eurasia would "promote separatism". This Eurasian Union would be a Russian Empire, and its Eurasian perspective invited co-operation and union with China and the Far East.

Putin has been influenced in his Eurasian outlook by the ultra-nationalist Russian philosopher Aleksandr Dugin, who has advocated Eurasianism and called on the Russian government to unite ethnic Russians and reject Western European values, another form of seeing the world as a Russian Slavophile rather than as a Westerniser (see p.132), and of cultivating a Eurasian perspective. Bound up in this perspective is the assumption that Russia is a new empire of ethnic Russians that will challenge the West.

Dugin was a keen supporter of Putin's war in Ukraine to restore the Kremlin's control over Ukrainians (ethnic Russians), and has been called "Putin's brain". He was so influential that his daughter, Darya Dugina, who spoke for her father's outlook on Russian TV, was killed in a car-bomb explosion on 21 August 2022, a terrorist act believed to have targeted Aleksandr Dugin, who until the last minute was going to accompany his daughter in the car with a bomb beneath it. Kyiv was immediately blamed, and the Russian FSB released pictures of Natalia Vovk of the Ukrainian secret service and of her driving a Mini Cooper to escape to Estonia.

Trade and pipeline corridors in Eurasia, and Russian dominance
Russia's dealings with Eurasia are the key to Russia's New World Order. The St Petersburg International Economic Forum revealed a challenge to the G7 of the industrialised West (which represents 12 per cent of the global population), from which Russia has been suspended: the new G8, four BRICS nations (Brazil, Russia, India, China) and Iran, Indonesia, Turkey and Mexico, whose GDP per purchasing parity power is already way above that of the old West-dominated G8. The BRICS+ (as it is referred to) was to be discussed at a summit in China (whose 'Three Rings' strategy developed geo-economic relations with its neighbours). Putin revealed that EU losses to sanctions against Russia could exceed $400 billion per year. In saying this, he again seemed to be challenging the Western New World Order.

President Tokayev of Kazakhstan, a partner of both Russia and China, said that Eurasian integration should progress hand-in-hand with China's Belt-and-Road Initiative (BRI). Eurasian integration has made possible interaction between the Eurasian Economic Union (EEU) and the Association of Southeast Asian Nations (ASEAN), "South-South co-operation".

Transportation corridors through Eurasia are very important to both Russia's Eurasian integration and China's Belt-and-Road Initiative (BRI). China's BRI developed along six corridors across Eurasia as well as the Maritime Silk Route from the South China Sea and Indian Ocean to Europe. It can now be seen that one of NATO's targets in its proxy war in Ukraine was to disrupt BRI corridors across Russia, just as under US occupation Afghanistan was prevented from offering a corridor to the BRI and INSTC (International North-South Transport Corridor, a 7,200km-long route for moving freight between Central Asia and Europe).

Russia has reclaimed the Black Sea ("historically Russian territory" according to Putin, now a "Russian lake"), and Russia's corridor to the Black Sea will greatly increase its sea trading prospects. Energy corridors competing for gas pipelines have been politicised by the South Stream, Nord Stream 1 and 2, TAPI (Turkmenistan–Afghanistan–Pakistan–India) and IPI (Iran–Pakistan–India) gas pipelines. In St Petersburg China and

India discussed the Northern Sea Route along the Russian coastline to the Barents Sea.

According to German intelligence, the three EU leaders (Macron, Scholz and the Italian President Mattarella) who visited Kyiv urged Zelensky to negotiate a surrender. Russia now looks like a military and energy superpower that has left the Western Syndicate ("the Western *élites*") helpless, and Eurasian corridors have contributed greatly to this new dominance. (Putin was in Vladivostok meeting North Korea's leader Kim Jong-un when I was in Moscow in 2019.)

Russia's taking back lands, the prospect of a Third World War or a further fall of the West

Russia's political dreams of a Russian New World order would include the countries Gorbachev lost in Eastern Europe. These could be won back by foreign conquest, perhaps a further Russian push into Odesa and beyond to Transnistria, Moldova and then Poland. But inextricably connected is Putin's Eurasian perspective and the "common economic space" from Lisbon to Vladivostok. When I first came across the "common economic space" I understood Putin to mean that he might join the EU and bring Russian territories to it. But looking back after Putin's invasion of Ukraine I now wonder if he meant that the Russian Empire of the Tsars should be enlarged to extend from Lisbon to Vladivostok in a Russian New World Order. This could be achieved by a nuclear strike with Russia's hypersonic Sarmat, which would reduce much of Western Europe to rubble. Otherwise, invading Poland would trigger the Third World War just as Hitler's invasion of Poland on 1 September 1939 as a "defensive" campaign to prevent Poles from allegedly persecuting ethnic Germans living in Poland triggered the Second World War.

Seemingly unaware of Sarmat, in December 2022 the US announced it was providing Ukraine with Patriot missiles, and in early January 2023 the UK announced it was providing 14 Challenger-2 tanks.

Dimitri Medvedev, deputy head of Putin's national security council, warned on 19 January 2023 that a Russian defeat in Ukraine could lead to a nuclear conflict.

Nikolai Patrushev, the Russian security council secretary and a close ally of Putin, said on 10 January 2023: "The events in Ukraine are not a clash between Moscow and Kyiv – this is a military confrontation between Russia and NATO, and above all the United States and Britain." Russia now regarded the war as a military confrontation with NATO, not as a likelihood of conflict with NATO as Medvedev had said on 12 May 2022, and in particular the two countries that had supplied the most arms to Ukraine, the US and UK.

What does the state of the Russia-Ukraine war tell us about the prospect of a Third World War or a further fall of the West? What is the likely outcome of the Russia-Ukraine war when it is seen from the perspective of August 2022? Between 1914 and 1945 150 million died, tens of millions were killed in wars, and the UN was established to set up a rules-based international order. Putin has violated this rules-based international order. The US and NATO do not want a Third World War but to preserve the rules-based international order they have helped Ukraine to defend itself. The war need not extend beyond Ukraine, but that is now Russia's choice. The US and NATO alliance will defend every inch of the NATO territories. Russia is not winning the war, but there is a war of attrition during which Russia has taken most of the Donbas in eastern Ukraine. This could turn into a stalemate, but Russia has given all the indications of preparing to push towards Odesa.

In no way – not operationally, tactically or strategically – has it been a successful war for Russia. Russia occupied Snake Island, which controls the passage of ships from Ukraine across the Black Sea, and there was Ukrainian military action with heavy artillery shells, and Russia chose to withdraw. The Western nations have increased their defence spending for it to be, in some cases, in excess of 2 per cent of GDP: the price of preserving freedom. But the Russians have capability, which is not just a question of the numbers of troops, tanks and planes, but also involves training of skills and techniques. The West is trying to match this capability by pouring money and arms into Ukraine. The Chinese also have capability, and plan to attack Taiwan at some time, at what it judges to be an opportune time.

By August 2022 the war of attrition in Ukraine was one in which

Russia was relying on its artillery superiority, on pounding cities into rubble. Russia was in control of Mariupol after a siege lasting two months, and was shelling Ukrainian positions across the southern regions of Zaporizhzhia, Kherson, Mykolaiv and Dnipropetrovsk. Russia began moving large numbers of troops to southern Ukraine in response to Ukraine's declared counter-offensive to liberate Kherson and Zaporizhzhia. After taking over Severodonetsk and Lysychansk, Russian troops controlled most of Luhansk region, and were pushing to take Sloviansk, Kramatorsk and Bakhmut. Putin had placed mines in Ukraine's seaports and prevented grain from leaving Ukraine, causing a food crisis for two years. Russia was reported to be giving Belarus nuclear missiles to upgrade its air force to counter the "aggressive" West, and also to be creating a land corridor from Russia to its exclave Kaliningrad.

Having taken the key cities, Russia looked as if it would keep Donbas. It looked as if the war would carry on. The head of the British army, Sir Patrick Sanders, said that Ukraine "is our 1937 moment" (meaning that the army must be fundamentally strengthened) and that Britain must be ready to "fight and win" to ward off the threat from Russia. The threat is a revival of a domineering Russia, and the expansion of Western troops was to deter Russia from further aggression in countries beyond Ukraine. Russia has threatened a nuclear strike. The West is always in high readiness, and has sought to keep the war below the nuclear threshold.

It looked as if Russia was winning, and that the West would avoid a Third World War and would undergo a further fall. The resignation of the UK's Prime Minister Boris Johnson, who had been supplying arms to Ukraine and had recklessly provoked Russia, was good news to those sensing that a Third World War could happen by accident, with British arms being blamed for Russian losses. It looked as if out of the war in Ukraine would come a new international order, and as if a Russian New World Order was being born.

As Russia captured a succession of pulverised cities during its progress in Ukraine's Donbas region in 2022, it looked as if the Russian New World Order was a golden phoenix that had risen from the ashes of the internal conflict at the end of the Soviet Union, and, starting on the new Mayan Year of the Phoenix on 22 April 2019, which I brought in, had begun to extend its lands at the beginning of a dream to extend its territorial presence from the Atlantic to the Pacific.

On a personal note I have described (see p.4 and in greater detail *Peace for our Time*, pp.30–57) how in 2015 I was invited to the World Philosophical Forum by Igor Kondrashin and found myself chairing a constitutional convention of more than 50 philosophers and bringing in the Universal State of the Earth, a World State based on paid membership (perhaps the method adopted by the Communist Party of the USSR) rather than on democratic principles. The Universal State of the Earth was based on classical Greek philosophy, which came out of a time when democracy was property-based and aristocratic and did not extend to women or slaves, and I entered into the spirit of a philosophical World State like Plato's ideal Republic rather than the spirit of a practical World State that could be set up today. I have described how I was made Chairman of the Supreme Council of Humanity, a position I was initially occupying until it could be offered to the then UN Secretary-General Ban Ki moon – I am still its Chairman now – and how I was fêted in Russia, addressed as "Your Excellency" and given awards.

Now, after Russia's invasion of Ukraine, I saw the Universal State of the Earth in a new light. Could this be the beginning of Russia's New World Order, had I 'inadvertently' (with my head full of philosophy, of Socrates saying "I am not an Athenian or a Greek, but a citizen of the world", and believing I was updating Plato's *Republic* in a contemporary constitution) brought in Russia's New World Order? Is Russia's New World Order going to be linked to the Universal State of the Earth, which I brought in?

I was particularly struck by a round-robin email Igor Kondrashin sent to members of the World Intellectual Forum, in which both he and I had been quiescent members (see pp.155–156): "Dear colleagues, I prefer not to listen and speak, but to read and write. Mr Pitroda, what I am involved now in is the formation of the Universal State of the Earth – the New World Order. It is very close to your subject – redesigning the world." (Sam Pitroda was in the World Intellectual Forum, see p.155, and had had a book published by

Penguin, *Redesign the World*.) Here was Igor describing the Universal State of the Earth I brought in as the New World Order. Russia's New World Order? It seemed that the Universal State of the Earth I brought in without a democratic structure and with a Communist-Party-style membership, and which was to be based one day in the Globe Center, perhaps in Crimea (see pp.4–5), was in fact the coming Russian New World Order. Igor then emailed me an electronic passport with 'Universal State of Earth' on the front cover, and inside I read 'Nationality: Supranational'. And I wondered whether we were now back to philosophy, with Socrates saying according to Plutarch in *De Exilio* (*On Exile*), "I am not an Athenian or a Greek but a citizen of the world" – in other words, supranational.

Igor forwarded to me an email he had sent to Kamala Harris, Biden's Vice-President, drawing her attention to the Universal State of the Earth, saying it was a ready-made New World Order, and asking if he could go to the White House and give a lecture on this New World Order that all should join. At the end were a number of names, including mine. His email to me arrived a month after Sam Pitroda had organised my first socialising Zoom conference for a supranational World State (see p.156), and I could not help thinking that Igor was parading his Russian New World Order, still officially based on classical philosophy, ahead of my supranational democratic partly-federal World State's New World Order.

In my mind I reconstructed a narrative of what might have happened between 2015 and 2022. Putin wanted a new Russian Universal State. I was chosen to front it as Igor and others wanted to keep a low profile. I chaired the founding of the Universal State of the Earth and was designated Head of Humanity (Chairman of the Supreme Council of Humanity). During the next year the Globe Center was designed, to be in Crimea, building to start in late 2016. In 2019 I was contacted to inaugurate a new world empire on the day of the new Year of the Phoenix, 22 April 2019. I inaugurated the new world empire, believing it would be the democratic World State I had outlined in *World State*, which I was to present to Putin and his advisers. It was in fact to be a Russian world empire, and it began with the invasion of Ukraine to destroy 30 US and NATO biological laboratories there. Putin wanted to bomb the biological laboratories and stop America's funding, arming and NATO-ising of Ukraine, and America's impeding the flow of gas from the Black Sea, and to connect Russia via Donbas to Transnistria. Putin had had a Russian Empire in mind on 22 April 2019, and while I spoke of an acceptable democratic World State I had described in my books, I might have been inadvertently bringing in Putin's Russian Empire, which might have been founded by me on 22 April 2019. Hence Sergey not washing his hands for three days because "they touched Hagger". Then I thought there was no evidence for any of this, it was speculative interpretation. Igor was still the supranational Igor I trusted.

But now I saw the Globe Center in a very different light. It was a meeting place for world delegates, and now, after Russia's invasion of Ukraine, as sinister as Hitler's Congress Hall or 'Colosseum' for 50,000 world delegates in Nuremberg, which I visited in October 1994[11] to do research for my epic poem on the Second World War, *Overlord*.

The structure for the Russian New World Order seemed to be there, but how many countries would send world delegates following Russia's invasion of Ukraine was a moot point. It now seemed a regional New World Order, like the Western New World Order for its 1 billion inhabitants, rather than a global New World Order for all humankind.

3. Possible Chinese New World Order
Chinese Belt-and-Road Initiative and trade surplus
In *The Fall of the West* I set out the rise of China through its Belt-and-Road Initiative (BRI), which is in 140 countries and semi-circles the West.[12] I also contrasted China's trade surplus in 2019 of $421.9 billion, and the US's trade deficit of $616.8 billion; and China's trade surplus in the first eleven months of 2020 of $460 billion with the US's trade deficit in 2020 of $678 billion, a gap of over $1 trillion per year.

According to the Centre for Economics and Business Research, by 2030 China will have overtaken the US as the world's largest economy. China's New World Order would be based on its economic power – in 2022 China's annual GDP growth was set to rise to 8 per cent – and its Belt-and-Road trade deals with many countries, building much-needed ports, airports and roads, and levelling up countries' infrastructure on terms beneficial to the host countries.[13]

China has threatened to invade Taiwan, and is expansionist. China has occupied islands in the South China Sea, including (from 1994) some of the islands in the Spratly Islands archipelago, which holds significant reserves of oil and natural gas and where Vietnam, Taiwan, the Philippines, Malaysia and Brunei also claim ownership of some islands. In a massive warlike parade to mark the 100th anniversary of the founding of the ruling Chinese Communist Party, President Xi declared before thousands of soldiers that China would not allow itself to be bullied, and that those who tried to bully China would face "broken heads and bloodshed in front of the iron Great Wall of the 1.4 billion Chinese people", a warning of coming war. Satellites showed that China was building 145 nuclear missile silos.[14] In mid-July 2022 the Chinese Communist Party had already made arrangements for its November 2022 Congress to appoint President Xi to a further five-year term in office and to give him the honorary title of "People's Leader". On 27 July 2022 in the course of a two-hour phone call President Xi told President Biden that China considers Taiwan to be an inalienable part of China (just as Putin considers Ukraine to be an inalienable part of Russia) according to a Chinese statement, and said: "Those playing with fire will get burnt."

Great-power rivalry between the US and China has endangered the rules-based multilateral order that has been operated by the UN, the World Trade Organization and international law since the Second World War. Competition and rivalry are displacing co-operation, and this is particularly the case between the EU and ASEAN (the Association of Southeast Asian Nations, a political and economic union of 10 member-states in Southeast Asia), which began a strategic partnership in December 2020. We are now living in a divided world, as during the Cold War when the UN was overshadowed by great-power rivalry.

Covid-19 broke out in China. I have examined its aetiology in *The Fall of the West* and found it began in 20 years of American gain-of-function research (1999–2019) in both the US and Wuhan, China. I have narrowed the outbreak to the Military World Games in Wuhan, which were opened by President Xi on 18 October 2019. Dozens of the 9,000 military athletes from 109 countries had Covid-like symptoms by the end of the Military World Games on 27 October 2019, and as Tehran's Parliament also had an outbreak shortly afterwards in February 2020, in which 10 per cent of the entire parliament were infected, I saw the outbreaks in Wuhan and Tehran as a covert American biological infection to undermine China's trade surplus and BRI, and to set back Iran's attempt to develop nuclear weapons.[15] I concluded in *The Fall of the West* that biological warfare had replaced nuclear warfare, and we were now in a new Biological Age.

Whatever its origin, Covid helped the US slow down China's BRI and temporarily reduce China's trade surplus as China's zero-tolerance Covid policy sent cities and regions into lockdown.

By 23 December 2022 there were 10,167,676 confirmed cases of Covid-19 in China with 31,585 deaths, according to the World Health Organisation. Estimates in January 2023 put the number of Chinese deaths at 1 million. It is not known whether biological warfare contributed to any or all of these. There were lockdowns in many cities. In November 2022 there was popular anger in China, ostensibly against lockdown but in fact directed at the Chinese Communist Party and President Xi, suggesting that a post-Communist China is waiting. China's union (stage 43 of the Chinese civilisation) had lasted since 1949, for 73 years; Russia's equivalent stage, the Soviet Union, lasted from 1917 to 1991, 74 years. China could be on the verge of breaking away from Communism as a result of the Covid restrictions, and could then be ready to join a global New World Order.

By the end of 2022 the Chinese New World Order was like a golden phoenix that had risen from the ashes of the internal conflict of the Cultural Revolution, which I personally discovered in March 1966.[16]

An authoritarian, Communist New World Order

If the Chinese Communist Party continues to be in power, China's New World Order would be authoritarian. On a personal note, I experienced an instance of how authoritarian this might be when an early copy of my *World Constitution* was worked on by a Chinese with legal knowledge who amended one of its 145 articles on the democratic power structure to give a rotational group leadership on the Chinese model, without bringing this to my attention. This Chinese wanted to publish *World Constitution* with amendments of which I was unaware, and present it as an authoritarian, not democratic, work.

It seemed that the Chinese New World Order would be a regional New World Order that applied to Communist China and territories it had absorbed, including Hong Kong. It would be based on China's Belt-and-Road Initiative in 140 countries, but would not be a truly global New World Order.

4. Possible Syndicate New World Order

The possible Western New World Order (no.1) may be brought into being by the Syndicate, in alliance with the Russian and Chinese New World Orders. The Syndicate's New World Order would not really be a fourth New World Order, but a variation with a different emphasis of the Western New World Order (no.1) that would include the Russian and Chinese New World Orders – or would be included within a Syndicate sell-out to Russia and China. It would be different from the Western New World Order (no.1), and so I am calling it no.4 even though it would really be a variation with a different emphasis of no.1.

We have, then, the Western, Russian and Chinese New World Orders, and a war in Ukraine that according to Biden's spokesman Ned Price (see p.96) would determine which New World Order would dominate. And behind the three possible regional New World Orders is the Syndicate.

The Syndicate dominated the US Federal Reserve from 1913,[17] the European central banks in Paris, Frankfurt, Vienna and Naples from the 18th and early 19th centuries and England's central bank from 1815, Russia's central bank after the 1917 Russian Revolution, and China's central bank from 1982,[18] and as I showed in *The Fall of the West* was levelling down the West and levelling up the East in preparation for a coming global New World Order it would control along with the 457 oil and gas pipelines in the world,[19] with sufficient freedom despite Schwab's technocratic governing methods to attract the democratic West and with sufficient authoritarianism to attract Eurasian-looking Russia and China in the East.

The Syndicate's multipolar Triple-Code New World Order

The descendants of the Syndicate's Rockefeller and Rothschild foundations and institutions were behind the West's, Russia's and

China's New World Orders to bring them within one New World Order based on Nelson Rockefeller's vision in 1962 and 1968 (see p.125)[20] that would resemble my Triple-Code badge (three circles in a triangular shape, see pp.48, 123). One of the three would be at the top, and the other two would be underneath – depending on the outcome of Russia's war in Ukraine and of China's progress in dominating world trade.

To see if the US's progress in arresting the decline and fall of the West, which is already at a new low following its hasty and Vietnam-like withdrawal from Afghanistan, put the US on top we should look back to 1991 and see the present world in context. In 1991 the US was supreme and the Soviet Union had collapsed. From one world superpower after 1991, the United States, the world has become multipolar with three superpowers – the US, the EU and China – all having spheres of influence. Now Russia is taking its place alongside them, making a fourth superpower.

Two of the superpowers, the US and the EU, are in alliance, and so are the other two: Russia, which is now looking towards Eurasia and is hostile to the West, and China, which is also hostile to the West. There are two Western superpowers that stand for liberalism, democracy and freedom, the US and the EU, and represent a democratic New World Order; and two authoritarian superpowers that are now expansionist and domineering and oppose the West, Russia and China, and both have New World Orders. And to prevent a Third World War these two alliances of superpowers must be restrained within a successor to the old UN's rule-based international order: the Syndicate's New World Order, in which one of the superpowers will predominate.

It has to be said that in mid-2022 of the three possible New World Orders, the West's has been under pressure and following its withdrawal from Afghanistan has been falling, and Russia has been fighting a war of attrition in Ukraine and does not look predominant, whereas China has been rising. It too has hypersonic intercontinental ballistic missiles.

In a Syndicate New World Order, China may become the dominant superpower, with (on the Triple-Code badge grouping) the West (the US and EU) and Russia beneath, perhaps because they will both have been damaged by nuclear strikes resulting from Russian expansionism following its war of attrition in Ukraine.

Would Russia carry out a first nuclear strike? The Syndicate would not want to turn the West into an unvisitable wasteland contaminated by radiation, but it might suit Russia or China to have key areas of the West (in Washington, London and Brussels) paralysed and unvisitable for 40 years. Deagel.com's forecasts seem to be based on nuclear strikes, and as the main intelligence supplier to the US, Deagel must have concluded that paralysing parts of the West, sealing the fall of the West and drastically reducing its population, is a credible and feasible scenario for a New World Order operating under the nuclear-striker (Russia or China).

What if the Western Syndicate has been covertly encouraging Russian individuals to invade Ukraine in order to defend Russian natural gas and oil, to cut Putin down to size, to level Russia down, so Ukraine becomes Russia's Suez, which involved an overreaching that levelled down the colonial British Empire? And what if Putin, weakened by the loss of 50,000 Russian troops and 4,000 tanks and the working of the Western Syndicate's levelling-down plan, nuclear-strikes his way out of being levelled down? Putin opposes Gorbachev's having given Russia's traditional sphere-of-influence countries like Poland to the West – hence he did not attend Gorbachev's funeral on 3 September 2022; and he opposes the West and NATO and still wants a Russian sphere of influence along Russia's borders with the West, and he may resist being levelled down by the war in Ukraine and may nuclear-strike his way to a Russian New World Order and hegemony over the West, as Deagel.com, the main supplier of intelligence to the US government, seems to have forecast.

And the same applies to China. Having had its BRI and expanding economy temporarily levelled-down by a pandemic for which it blames the US, it may too nuclear-strike the West to paralyse it and extend China's New World Order and hegemony into the rest of the visitable world.

These drastic scenarios can be avoided if China and Russia can be persuaded to take part along with a levelled-down West in a Syndicate New World Order.

China, that has absorbed Hong Kong and may also absorb Taiwan by conquest, brooks no dissent at present, and although its people may be longing for freedom under its authoritarian Communist system, it may be willing to share a future Syndicate partnership organised by 'Rothschilds' who took control of the People's Bank of China in 1982.[21]

Russia may be willing to share a future Syndicate partnership organised by 'Rothschilds', who owned the Russian central bank after the 1917 Russian Revolution.[22] As we have seen on p.144, 'Rothschilds' have also owned or controlled the US Federal Reserve, the Bank of England (ownership of which is sometimes reported as being the UK Government's, the Treasury Solicitor's on behalf of HM Treasury), central banks in key European countries and China's central bank. In short, the common factor in a Syndicate New World Order is 'Rothschilds', who are crucial to funding all three New World Orders, and China may be on top in the Syndicate's Triple-Code New World Order, with the West and Russia beneath. It would be an authoritarian New World Order, one compounded by Schwab's technocracy, until the oppressed Chinese crave for freedom and rebel and democratise the authoritarian New World Order, introduce democratic structures that allow more freedom like Gorbachev's *glasnost* (openness in communication and information) and Western values, including the values of the UN's rules-based international order.

The Syndicate New World Order would be imposed on the world from behind the scenes for commercial reasons, and as it is planned that its stakeholder companies would run the world and ownership would be removed from everyone to bring in a global Communism, and people's brains would be tinkered with digitally to control their thoughts, it would not be a New World Order that humankind will have chosen. Rather it would be an authoritarian one that has been imposed on humankind so the Syndicate's *élites* can prosper at the expense of humankind.

5. Possible supranational, multipolar New World Order

But there is another way, a global way that treats the West (the US and EU), Russia and China equally and constructively builds on the fall of the West so the West takes its place in a united world as a participant rather than as the dominant force and preserves its centuries of history and tradition without having them reduced to rubble by hypersonic missiles. It is a way 'Rothschilds' and the Syndicate can be involved in without dominating behind the scenes, a way that includes all the four previous possible New World Orders but without the dehumanising of Schwab's Syndicate technocracy and mind control.

It is a global way I have devised in three of my Universalist works, have put forward and have now been asked to be involved in: a supranational world government within a partly-federal World State with legal powers to fulfil seven goals for the benefit of all humankind, including all Americans, Europeans, Russians and Chinese. This approach bypasses a Syndicate New World Order that includes four superpowers, a levelled-down West and a rising, rampant East and the semi-servitude of all humankind.

The end of US hegemony

At present, without this global way, the world is facing a nuclear catastrophe because of a Western narrative that the West is noble, that the US hegemony is unchangeable, and Russia and China are autocracies attempting to erode American security and prosperity.

This narrative is a partial manipulation of the facts.[23] Since 1980 the US has fought at least 15 overseas wars by choice, including wars in Afghanistan, Iraq, Libya, Panama, Serbia, Syria and Yemen, whereas China has fought none and Russia one beyond the former Soviet Union (in Syria). This tally excludes Russia's actions in ex-Soviet Chechnya, Georgia and Ukraine. In 2022 the US had military bases in 85 countries, China in three countries (but a Belt-and-Road-Initiative presence in 140 countries) and Russia in one country beyond the former Soviet Union (Syria).

The US's hegemonic condemnation of Chinese and Russian autocratic authoritarianism is behind the Western narrative since 1980. Just as George W. Bush presented Islamic fundamentalism as being autocratic without mentioning the CIA's creation of jihadists in Afghanistan (which was preceded by a CIA operation to provoke a Soviet invasion of Afghanistan) and in Syria (which was preceded by a CIA operation in 2011 to overthrow Assad), so Biden has been presenting China and Russia as making economies less free, growing their militaries, controlling information and expanding their influence. US House of Representatives Speaker Nancy Pelosi's visit to Taiwan on 2 August 2022 was provocative but the G7 only condemned China's reaction, and the West promised Gorbachev that NATO would not enlarge to the east and then enlarged to the east in four waves in 1999, incorporated three Central-European countries in 2004 and seven more countries including some in the Black-Sea region and the Baltic states in 2008, committed to enlarge NATO in Ukraine after overthrowing Yanukovych in 2014 (see p.79), and in Georgia, and in 2022 invited four Asian-Pacific leaders to NATO to form an alliance against China.

NATO has subverted the Minsk international agreements to end the war in the Donbas region of Ukraine. The first agreement was signed on 5 September 2014 by Ukraine, Russia and the OSCE (Organization for Security and Co-operation in Europe) and the Donetsk and Luhansk People's Republics, following mediation by France and Germany, and established a buffer zone between Ukraine and the two republics. This failed to stop the fighting, and the second agreement, an update, was signed on 12 February 2015 and provided self-government to certain areas of Donbas and gave the Ukrainian government control of the state border. On 21 February 2022 Putin recognised the Donetsk and Luhansk republics and on 22 February 2022 declared that the Minsk agreements "no longer existed".

In Ukraine, France and Germany, the guarantors of the Minsk II agreement, failed to press Ukraine to carry out its commitments, and the US sent vast armaments to Ukraine for the war (see pp.84–85) and refused to negotiate with Putin over the enlargement of NATO in Ukraine (see p.65). NATO's narrative that it is defensive ignores the CIA operations in Afghanistan and Syria, the NATO bombing of Serbia in 1999, NATO's overthrow of Gaddafi of Libya in 2011, NATO's occupation of Afghanistan for 15 years, Biden calling for Putin to be ousted, and US Defense Secretary Lloyd Austin stating that the US war aim in Ukraine is the weakening of Russia.

The US, which has 4.2 per cent of the world's population and 16 per cent of the world's GDP, is attempting to remain the world's hegemonic power and maintain a world hegemony even though the

GDP of the G7 is less than that of the BRICS countries (Brazil, Russia, India, China and South Africa), and the G7 has 6 per cent of the world's population whereas the BRICS countries have 41 per cent of the world's population. If the US were to decide to co-operate with the rest of the world by supporting a supranational, democratic, partly-federal World State rather than to continue to pursue hegemony and conflict that could result in a nuclear catastrophe, then the US would avoid war with China and Russia and enable the world to face its energy, food and social crises (the crises in the seven areas of a partly-federal World State). The European leaders can improve global security by respecting the security arrangements of all European nations, including both Ukraine and Russia, and by working for the non-enlargement of NATO and the implementation of the Minsk II agreement (the second Minsk agreement).

Setting up a democratic world government within a partly-federal, multipolar World State confined to seven goals

Setting up a democratic world government within a partly-federal World State is based on my three works *The World Government* (2010), *World State* (2018) and *World Constitution* (2018). The objective is to create a democratic supranational world government with sufficient authority and legal powers to solve all the world's problems within seven areas, leaving all nation-states as they are internally and, except for the seven areas, internationally.

As we have seen, the international situation has become urgent following Russia's invasion of Ukraine and its attack on the UN's post-1945 rules-based international order, and there have been threats that a Third World War is about to start. The world has seemingly unsolvable problems that have impacted on all humankind:

1. wars and nuclear weapons (162 wars between 1945 and 2017 and around 40 ongoing wars in 2021, and 12,705 nuclear warheads in January 2022, around 2,000 of which are in active readiness including hypersonic intercontinental ballistic missiles that can destroy a country within three minutes), and seemingly no prospect of progress in voluntary disarmament;

2. shortage of resources and energy, poverty and hunger;
3. environmental problems such as global warming and famine;
4. self-perpetuating disease including the Covid pandemic;
5. lack of access to education, science and skills development;
6. an inadequate world economy and consequent financial and funding crises; and
7. a lack of spiritual and ethical awareness compounded by friction between religions that make wars more likely.

These problems are interconnected, and solving them would release funds to build peaceful communities. The saving of the total military expenditure in 2022 of $2.113 trillion alone would cover the cost of setting up a supranational world government that would have legal powers to solve the seven problems supranationally. The UN works at an international level by persuasion and does not have the legal authority to solve the world's problems supranationally. It needs a supranational 'add-on' to solve them within a democratic framework.

In my scheme, a supranational, multipolar government would unite all nation-states federally at the level of seven goals while all nation-states would continue to be separate internally and (apart from the seven communal areas of the seven goals) internationally. The world government would be confined to seven goals within seven areas:

1. Creating supranational legal powers to abolish and end war, keep a rules-based peace with human rights between nation-states with the aid of a world peace-keeping force, and achieve universal disarmament for the benefit of all humankind;
2. Sharing resources and energy supplies, and redistributing wealth to eliminate poverty and hunger and to supply basic needs for the benefit of all humankind;
3. Solving environmental problems caused by climate change such as global warming and famine while respecting all life forms and avoiding violent farming methods, for the benefit of all humankind;
4. Ending disease, including eradicating Covid, and promoting wellness and good health in all for the benefit of all humankind;

5. Extending education, science and skills development for the benefit of all humankind;

6. Delivering a growing world economy and solving all financial and funding crises for the benefit of all humankind; and

7. Raising awareness of universal spirituality and global ethics, and ending all friction between religions so all religious leaders can co-operate, for the benefit of all humankind.

The structure of the supranational, multipolar authority is in the chart on p.183. At the international level there would be a directly-elected democratic Lower House, a World Parliamentary Assembly, initially with 815 seats and eventually (when 26 currently dependent and 9 disputed territories can be represented) 850 seats. Initially the World Parliamentary Assembly could be housed in the US General Assembly a few days a month as it is phased in. The UN Security Council would become a veto-less World Executive Council.

At the supranational level there would be a directly-elected Upper House, a World Senate with 92 senators in 46 zonal seats (2 per zonal seat); a World Commission which would operate like the European Commission; a World Council of Ministers with 29 World Departments; and a World President elected every four years.

The UN Secretary-General would be an important link between the international and supranational levels as he or she would oversee the World Parliamentary Assembly and report upwards to the World Senate's World Peace Enforcement Committee (see chart) which would in turn report upwards to the World Senate. Over a period of time the UN General Assembly would be replaced by the World Parliamentary Assembly and General Assembly.

The structure would be that of a partly-federal, multipolar, democratic World State, *partly* federal because it would have just seven goals. The representatives of the legislative Lower House, the World Parliamentary Assembly, would pass the legal powers to set up a World State, and the Upper House, the World Senate, and the World President would approve them in a democratic way. In the same way, the legislative Lower House would confirm the World State's legal power to implement the seven goals, and the Upper House, the World

Senate, and World President would approve the limits of the World State's partly-federal powers.

In a letter of 14 July 2022 to 14 UN Ambassadors, Dr Klaus Schlichtmann (Nobel Peace Prize nominee, 2022), working jointly with Kazutoshi Abe, the former Prime Minister of Japan who was assassinated on 8 July 2022, sought to abolish the Japanese Constitution's "war-abolishing" Article 9 because "UN Member States have failed to respond to the plea to abolish war as an institution and take legislative action to establish 'an international peace based on justice and order'". The letter ends: "Limiting or transferring sovereign powers to the UN in a legislative act is precisely what the [UN] Charter and the United Nations intended." In a later letter of 18 July 2022 to the same 14 UN Ambassadors he concluded with President Bush's words in his speech to the UN General Assembly on 1 October 1990: "Not since 1945 have we seen the real possibility of using the United Nations as it was designed, as a center for international collective security." The partly-federal World State I have outlined is just this, a centre for international collective security – following a legislative act to limit or transfer sovereign powers.

The World State, a republic, would be called The United Federation of the World from a line in Tennyson's 'Locksley Hall' (1842): "In the Parliament of man, the Federation of the World." It would be known as the UF for short, an abbreviation that suggestively echoes the UN. The word 'United' suggestively incorporates the United States besides echoing the United Nations, and the word 'Federation' suggestively incorporates the Federation of Russia.

This is an ideal form of world government as it is a realistic and gradual process that takes account of the existing system. As a supranational 'add-on' with an important future link role for the UN Secretary-General, it may be acceptable to the UN as a basis for further study.

In my work *The World Government* there are eight possible models for a world Government. In *World State* the eighth model is presented as the ideal for a World State. The allocation of seats in the Lower and Upper Houses is based on the UN's 2016 projections of world population figures of the nation-states as percentages of the world population.

Size of territories, nuclear influence, Permanent Membership of the UN Security Council and world influence were also taken into account in 133 pages of evidence and data. My world constitution is set out as 145 articles in 14 chapters in *World Constitution*, and 26 constitutional precedents and 204 constitutions were consulted. My supranational 'add-on' scheme is based on extensive research.

Many have called for a world government, including Truman, Einstein, Churchill, Eisenhower, Gandhi, Russell, J.F. Kennedy and Gorbachev (to whom I gave signed copies of *World State* and *World Constitution* via his consultant Vladimir Polyakov in Moscow in April 2019, see p.38).

What will happen next, can the UN convert itself into being part of a supranational, multipolar World State?
Realistically, what will happen next? The West, though united while the Russia-Ukraine war is still being fought, may be divided as soon as Putin asks for a cease-fire so a negotiation can begin, in which parts of Ukraine become Russian.

The UN has been unable to keep the peace; hence the 162 wars between 1945 and 2017. Can it convert itself into a partly-supranational, democratic world government within a partly-federal World State confined to seven areas? If so, the West could bring together the other Eastern superpowers into a democratic World Parliamentary Assembly and a World Senate, and the West's rules-based values would be perpetuated. If this does not happen, and Russia's war of attrition continues, there may be a Third World War ahead, and an authoritarian Syndicate New World Order with a subordinate West that may have been pulverised and nuclear-attacked, as America's most secret intelligence agency Deagel.com has forecast (the US population down from 327 million to under 100 million, UK down from 66 million to 15 million, Germany down from 81 million to 28 million and France down from 67 million to 39 million):[24] a West that has undergone a further fall and is no longer a senior partner in the coming authoritarian New World Order.

The hope is that if this happens, eventually it will turn itself into a freedom-loving New World Order, as the peoples of Russia and China tire of being dictated to, rebel and opt for a free, democratic way of life. If a supranational partly-federal democratic World State cannot be created with the help of the UN now, it will emerge after a spell of authoritarian New-World-Order rule.

But it does not have to be like that, there is a better way – so long as the UN can be persuaded to go along with a supranational world government.

My involvement in setting up a supranational, multipolar World State

I began on a personal note, describing how I brought in the Universal State of the Earth in 2015 (see p.4), and it is appropriate to end on a personal note. Having been personally involved in bringing in a possible Russian New World Order, the Universal State of the Earth, I was now personally involved in bringing in my supranational democratic world government and World State, which I had set out in *The World Government, World State* and *World Constitution*, a possible fifth New World Order.

I had been invited to join the Executive Board of the World Intellectual Forum on 6 July 2020 after being asked for a summary of *The World Government*, and had agreed. I was too busy with my books to do much until 2022. I was then asked to give a Zoom presentation on *The World Government, World State* and *World Constitution* at the annual meeting, and I spoke on the need for supranationalism and outlined my coming World State, a democratic partly-federal World State. My supranational approach went down well, and I was asked to chair a working group that would put into action the idea I ended my presentation with: that a Forum's working group should ask the UN to set up a working group on the feasibility of a democratic world government within a partly-federal World State confined to seven goals.

Sam Pitroda, an Indian entrepreneur living in Chicago and author of a Penguin book, *Redesign the World* (see p.139), said he would assist me. A plan was swiftly drawn up. I would set up a working group of five immediately, under my leadership; and I would draw up a draft preliminary document and plan of action. There would be nine conferences throughout the world, beginning with India, Africa, the EU, Mexico and the US, and having obtained reaction to the document I would hold a press conference to launch a new website with a link for public feedback. I would then lead a group that would meet the UN Secretary-General armed with the public reaction, and, following a presentation, request that a UN working group should be set up to work on a world government through a partly-federal supranational World State, and that the World Intellectual Forum would liaise with the UN working group and have an input.

At the first meeting of the World Intellectual Forum working group I was asked as Chairman to prepare a formal Proposal to set up a supranational world government as a document that could be turned into a PowerPoint presentation and be socialised at nine conferences. Sam asked for it "tomorrow". I began work on the Proposal on global good governance that would be the basis for a PowerPoint presentation and finished it the following day, and it is in Appendix 2 together with a chart on the structure of a partly-federal World State. Sam had rung a friend who worked very near the office of the UN Secretary-General, and was told that only governments could request a presentation to the UN Secretary-General. He told Sam how this could be done, and Sam undertook to organise a presentation as he knew a number of world leaders. There was now a prospect that my supranational New World Order could replace the four other possible New World Orders and incorporate them into my own scheme.

Sam oversaw the turning of my Proposal on global good governance into a PowerPoint presentation, and his presentation included the idea that each state of the 193 UN nation-states should have a minister responsible for seven goals who would be in charge of seven sub-ministries, one for each goal, who would all report to the world government and to my working group, and seven global domain experts to find technological solutions. My working group would have its own seven groups of global domain experts and advisers. These technical experts would solve the seven problems relating to the seven goals without the involvement of political bosses. This led me to wonder in an email to Sam whether we should ask the UN to recognise our working group as a working group that can report to the UN General

Assembly rather than ask the UN to set up their working group – and if the UN would help organise the nation-states' funding of the ministers, seven sub-ministries and domain experts, and the seven groups of global domain experts who would advise our working group.

Sam had a foundation registered in the UK as a 501C non-profit foundation with federal tax exemption which he could change to our foundation. I asked him to speak to his contact in the Rockefeller Foundation to see if his foundation could receive funds from the Rockefeller Foundation that would pay the salaries of the domain experts. Our working group and the World Intellectual Forum would operate as projects or satellites of his foundation, which should have a name that signified its mission and attract funding: the Supranational Foundation, or the Federation of the World Foundation.

I held the first socialising conference with Indian intellectuals on 28 July 2022. I spoke about my journey and then my Universalism and then talked the Indian group (all of high calibre in government or trade) through the PowerPoint presentation. I then gave a summary, in the course of which I said that our working group, the only one working on a supranational world government, could be considered by the UN to be a steering group worth funding to issue a report, and that if people in high places saw the urgency and the benefit, then the UN might consider adopting our working group and requesting it to write a report to the UN General Assembly. I asked for the group's reaction: whether we should make a presentation in high places and whether our project was worth some funding from an institution or foundation. The response of the group was very favourable. There would initially be four more such conferences with different parts of the world (Africa, the EU, Mexico and the US). Sam told me he would be mentioning our project informally to the President of the Rockefeller Foundation in two weeks' time.

In mid-August Sam spoke to the President of the Rockefeller Foundation, Rajiv Shah about our project. The Rockefeller Foundation were behind the setting up of the UN. The UN's headquarters were built on Rockefellers' land, and Rockefellers paid the salaries of UN employees during the 1940s. The relationship between the Rockefeller Foundation and the UN Secretary-General is very close. On 8 September 2022 the

UN General Assembly passed a Resolution, to set up The Summit of the Future[25] to strengthen global governance "for a better tomorrow" in New York on 22 and 23 September 2024, along the lines of the working group on global governance I was chairing.

Had the video of my presentation on global governance to India been passed via the Rockefeller Foundation to the UN, and was the UN Resolution influenced by my presentation on 28 July 2022?

Then, on Saturday 8 October 2022 I was emailed by Anton Serov, a youngish man from Moscow's time zone who described himself as "a journalist currently working as a freelance news contributor with Den TV". I believed that Den TV was Indian-owned. He asked me to do a Zoom video interview on some of my books for an hour. I thought it would be going out to India. He sent me nine written questions about my books *The Syndicate* (2004) and *The Algorithm of Creation* (setting out my Theory of Everything, due out in 2023), and on my meeting with Ezra Pound in 1970 and my BRICS silver medal for 'Vision for Future'. He wanted to do the interview the following day, Sunday 9 October 2022, and when I connected at 3pm and asked where our interview would be viewed, he said, "Throughout Russia." He said there would be an interpreter and perhaps subtitles.

I was surprised, but went along with what turned out to be a two-hour interview, mostly on the future redesigned world order that Russia could enter after the present difficulties. I outlined a supranational, multipolar New World Order in which the US, EU, China and Russia would be equal. I spoke on how my supranational, multipolar World State would be a way forward for Russia, how the seven goals and new legal powers of the partly-federal world government would transform Russia's future, how my World State would benefit all humankind, for whom it is important to have humanitarian feelings, and how wars do not benefit anybody. I said, "Look at Hitler in the ruins of Berlin in 1945."

At the end he asked, "What message have you for the Russian people?"

I said, "Beneath all conflicts is unity, all opposites are reconciled in an underlying harmony." (I was thinking of the algebraic formula $+A + -A = 0$ that reconciles all opposites in a unity and features in all my works.) I said that in the future Russia could join a redesigned, multipolar New World Order in which it would be equal alongside the US, EU and China. That would be a fresh start, and that as the Queen said, "We'll meet again." I spoke at length about Russia's traditional culture, and about Dostoevsky, Tolstoy, Turgenev and Solzhenitsyn.

Then he said, "Who would you like the video of this interview to go to?"

I said, "President Putin, or one of his assistants."

For two hours I had made it very clear indirectly that Russia would be changing its course to a multipolar New World Order that would offer a better future for the world's, including Russia's, grandchildren.

That night, no doubt unaware of my video as it was still being translated into Russian and perhaps subtitled, Putin ordered some hundred missiles to rain down on numerous Ukrainian cities, including Kyiv, to express his displeasure at the bomb-damage done to the Kerch Strait Bridge that joined Russia and Crimea.

About three weeks later David Lorimer sent me a speech Putin made at the Russian Club Valdai on 24 October, on respect for cultures.[26] In it Putin called for a multipolar New World Order in which Russia would be equal. He spoke at length on traditional Russian culture, and mentioned Dostoevsky in some detail, quoting from *The Possessed*, and Solzhenitsyn at some length. He said, "The centres of the multipolar international order and the West will have to start a dialogue on an equal footing about a common future for us all, and the sooner the better." He said, "We are hoping that pragmatism will triumph and Russia's dialogue with the genuine, traditional West as well as with other co-equal development centres, will become a major contribution to the construction of a multipolar world order."

Could Putin have been told about, or listened directly to, what I said?

So in the middle of my assessing the outcome of the conflict of the West (the US and EU) with Russia and China, and the differing New World Orders ahead and the possibility of a Syndicate 'Triple-Code' New World Order, I suddenly found that I was promoting my own global non-Syndicate New World Order based on a supranational multipolar world government within a democratic partly-federal World State. Having begun this book as an observer, a spectator, I now found that by the end of the book I had become a player with a supranational New World Order that avoided the authoritarian elements of the other four New World Orders.

And so once again I call on President Putin, who along with President Biden has been given signed copies of my *World State* and *World Constitution* by an adviser (Putin in 2019, Biden in 2021, see p.122), to do as I said in my letters to Putin (see pp.12–14 and 35–38) and abandon nationalism for supranationalism and work with me and a UN working group to get to the UN General Assembly and lay a model of a multipolar World State before it to solve all problems. And I call on President Biden to follow President Obama's example and ban gain-of-function research in all countries – in the US and in China and in Ukraine – and support me in appealing to the UN General Assembly to consider a democratic partly-federal World State as the way forward for the world (notwithstanding Guterres' partnership with Schwab), and bring in with it a new world empire of peace. I urge President Biden to get together with Presidents Putin and Xi and bring in a supranational partly-federal New World Order that still leaves humans as humans and not semi-robotic machines.

In *The Promised Land* I described how at 80 Moses looked down from Mount Nebo at the promised land he would never enter, and I now knew that at 83 I could be leading some of the key leading figures in our age up Mount Nebo to show them a promised land of milk and honey that I would never enter. I would be showing the promised land during a PowerPoint presentation to India, Europe, America and Africa, and elsewhere, and, given my years, would have done my duty and all that could reasonably be expected of me.

I would continue to parade my supranational, multipolar, partly-federal democratic World State with seven goals that would make the world a safer place. I was born in May 1939, three-and-a-bit months before the Second World War was declared on 1 September 1939, and I cannot help wondering if I was sent down by the angels to experience the war, live under the flight of the flying bombs, the doodle-bugs and V-2 rockets, and come up with a solution that will make future wars of this kind illegal and impossible. I sometimes feel I have to do this before I return to whence I came, and in that spirit I will carry on explaining my supranational New World Order whose partly-federal World State's World Commission will sit, as on my Triple-Code badge, above its Lower and Upper Houses, its World Parliamentary Assembly and World Senate, and also above the Western alliance between the US and EU and the Eastern alliance between Russia and China, and the Syndicate's dehumanising merging of the two – above all the other four possible New World Orders.

The Golden Phoenix

And so at 83, I seemed to have trumped the four other possible New World Orders. My supranational, multipolar New World Order sits above the Western democratic and technocratic New World Order and the Eastern authoritarian New World Order of Russia supporting China on my Triple-Code triangular grouping, which the Syndicate is planning to unite, and is above them all like a Golden Phoenix that has risen from the ashes of world chaos and war and the seven problems the UN has been unable to solve, and it overhangs the world like the new Year of the Phoenix which I brought in on 22 April 2019.

In Moscow I had received the Golden Phoenix which had once been the stamp of the Rothschilds, and now I was seeking to implement a partly-federal, democratic World State with seven goals and its New World Order in place of the Syndicate's Triple-Code authoritarian New World Order, 'Rothschilds' central-bank New World Order. I was seeking to implement a New World Order that has risen from the ashes of the West's Second World War and recent decline and should be known as the 'Golden Phoenix' New World Order. And the West's US and EU, Russia and China would all be participating democratically, so arranging them within a 'Triple Code' so one dominated the other two would no longer be a consideration. My supranational 'Golden Phoenix' New World Order would have replaced 'Rothschilds'' Syndicate New World Order, and the chart on p.183 shows 'Rothschilds'' Bilderberg Group reporting upwards to the World Senate's World Openness Committee.

The Golden Phoenix was now above all its contenders and being socialised round the world. It has risen from the ashes of war – the Second World War and 162 other wars and now Russia's war in

Ukraine – and from the ashes of the Syndicate's attempts to turn humans into automata (the Western Reset New World Order) and slaves (the Russian and Chinese New World Orders). It hangs in the sky, glorious, golden, a new world empire that began in 2019, which I brought in: the United Federation of the World with the seven feathers of its wings denoting the seven world problems and the seven goals. It hangs in the sky as a symbol of the universal peace it can bring in, the seven feathers on its wings also symbolising the seven main disciplines and the seven branches of literature which represent Universalism's approach to the fundamental unity of the universe and humankind, uniting all New World Orders and different disciplines into one golden future of peace and prosperity: a Golden Age.

Timeline

List of dates of key events relating to *The Golden Phoenix*

31 Oct 2004	Presidential election in Ukraine, pro-Russian Viktor Yanukovych declared to have defeated pro-European Viktor Yushchenko despite having fewer votes.
Nov–Dec 2004	Orange Revolution.
10 Jan 2005	Viktor Yushchenko declared the winner of the re-run ballot and inaugurated as President on 23 January 2005.
17 Jan 2010	Presidential election won by Viktor Yanukovych.
2010	Putin's vision of a "common economic space" stretching from Lisbon to Vladivostok.
2012	Enormous gas reserves discovered in Ukraine's share of the Black Sea and in eastern Ukraine.
2013	Royal Dutch Shell starts drilling.
Dec 2013	US investment of over $5 billion in Ukraine confirmed.
Feb 2014	Conflict between Russia and Ukraine.
Mar 2014	Russia's annexation of Crimea.
7 Oct 2015	NH invited to attend the World Philosophical Forum's annual meeting in Athens and brings in the Universal State of the Earth.
3 Oct 2016	At the World Philosophical Forum's next annual meeting, NH shown an image of the Globe Center, the HQ of the Universal State of the Earth planned to be built in Crimea.
23 Nov 2016	NH receives Gusi Peace Prize for Literature in Manila.
29 Jun 2018	*World State* and *World Constitution* published.
22 Apr 2019	NH's speech in Civic Chamber, Moscow brings in a new Year of the Phoenix and the Supranational New World Order; NH receives the Russian Ecological Foundation's golden-phoenix lapel

	badge and BRICS silver medal.
23 Apr 2019	NH receives silver medal showing Vernadsky from the Russian Academy of Natural Sciences.
24 Apr 2019	NH visits Gorbachev's consultant Vladimir Polyakov.
25 Apr 2019	NH gives a two-hour TV interview and visits the Union of Russian Writers, is made a member and receives a membership badge.
26 Apr 2019	NH plants the first of the Mayor of Moscow's 193 Siberian cedars to be planted in each of the UN's 193 nation-states, and the first of a million to be planted in Russia, and meets the chairman of Moscow City Duma, a meeting shown on Russian TV.
27 Apr 2019	NH visits the Kremlin's Cathedral of the Archangel.
28 Apr 2019	NH at Igor Kondrashin's *dacha* and is later given a personal concert at Barvikha sanatorium, Putin's rest-house.
29 Apr 2019	NH hands over signed copies of *World State* and *World Constitution* for Putin and three of his assistants.
30 Apr 2019	NH leaves Russia.
13 Jun 2019	World Economic Forum (Schwab) and UN (Guterres) sign Strategic Partnership Framework to accelerate the implementation of the UN's 2030 Agenda for Sustainable Development.
3 Jun 2020	The World Economic Forum's The Great Reset announced by Schwab and Prince Charles.
Mar–Apr 2021	Build-up of Russian troops on Ukraine's border.
Jul 2021	Putin's essay 'On the Historical Unity of Russians and Ukrainians'.
Oct 2021–Feb 2022	Build-up of Russian troops in Russia and Belarus.
16 Nov 2021	NH signs copies of *World State* and *World Constitution* for Biden, and posts them the next day.
17 Dec 2021	Putin demands that the US and NATO should agree

	Ukraine will never join NATO and will withdraw from NATO member states in Eastern Europe.
24 Feb 2022	Putin invades Ukraine.
24 Feb 2022	Ned Price, Biden's spokesman, says that Russia and China want a world order that would be illiberal, and that the Russia-Ukraine war would determine who will rule the coming world order.
Feb–May 2022	US invests over $3 billion in weapons for Ukraine.
8 Mar 2022	Victoria Nuland admits Ukraine has biological research facilities.
11 Mar 2022	Statement by Vassily Nebenzia (Russia's representative to the UN) that Ukraine developed 30 biological laboratories not accepted by the other 14 members of the UN Security Council.
21 Mar 2022	Biden says there is a coming new world order and the US must lead it.
10 May–29 Jul 2022	NH writes *The Golden Phoenix*.
11 May 2022	Briefing by Ministry of Defence of the Russian Federation on biological weapons in Ukraine.
12 May 2022	Medvedev speaks of the likelihood of nuclear war.
23–26 May 2022	World Economic Forum's annual gathering at Davos.
9 Jun 2022	Putin compares himself to Peter the Great.
15–18 Jun 2022	St Petersburg International Economic Forum, addressed by Putin on 17 June 2022.
24 Jun 2022	NH's presentation on a supranational world government to the World Intellectual Forum.
4 Jul 2022	First meeting of World Intellectual Forum's working group chaired by NH.
28 Jul 2022	NH's PowerPoint presentation to India for the World Intellectual Forum.
24 Jun 2022	NH gives a presentation to the World Intellectual Forum on a supranational, multipolar world government and partly-federal World State and New World Order.
4 Jul 2022	NH is asked to chair a working group on

	global good governance.
Mid-Aug 2022	Sam Pitroda meets Rajiv Shah, President of the Rockefeller Foundation.
28 Jul 2022	NH gives a PowerPoint slide presentation on a partly-federal, democratic World State and multipolar New World Order to India.
8 Sep 2022	UN General Assembly Resolution to strengthen global governance and prepare for The Summit of the Future on 22 and 23 September 2024.
23–27 Sep 2022	Putin holds four referendums and annexes Luhansk, Donetsk, Zaporizhzhia and Kherson regions.
25–28 Sep 2022	Four Nord Stream 1 and 2 pipelines sabotaged and put out of action.
9 Oct 2022	NH interviewed by Anton Serov to go out over "the whole of Russia", speaks of traditional Russian culture and calls on Russia to enter a multipolar New World Order as an equal multipolar centre and end the war with Ukraine.
24 Oct 2022	Putin speaks at Club Valdai on traditional Russian culture and calls for a multipolar New World Order as an equal multipolar centre.
Mid-Nov 2022	Kherson evacuated, Russian troops withdraw to the River Dnipro's eastern bank.

Appendices

Appendix 1

Résumé of Nicholas Hagger's Intentions Regarding
World State/World Constitution Initiative and Project (2017)

An approach to the UK Government

1. Project

This project is an innovative and exclusively UK initiative that looks beyond UK-EU relations to the UK's post-Brexit global role.

The aim of the project is to bring to the world's attention my call for a democratic, partly-federal World State to solve the world's problems fundamentally, as outlined in *World State* and *World Constitution*. The UN is not strong enough to achieve this under the present system: it has failed to prevent 162 wars since 1945 (see *World State*, p.288) and 72 current wars (see *World State*, p.268), and there are 14,900 nuclear weapons (see *World State*, p.294).

Under a World State each nation-state would remain the same internally and, initially, externally but would agree to a partly-federal body having supranational control of seven areas to solve all the world's current problems. In implementing the seven goals it would:

- bring peace between nation-states, and disarmament;
- share natural resources and energy so that all humankind can have a raised standard of living;
- solve environmental problems such as global warming;
- end disease;
- end famine;
- solve the world's financial crisis; and
- redistribute wealth to eliminate poverty.

There would be an elected lower house, a World Parliamentary Assembly with 850 representatives (for composition see *World State*, p.166), and an elected upper house, a World Senate (for composition see *World State*, p.179). See the diagram on *World State*, p.173 [see an updated version in *The Golden Phoenix*, p.183] for the structure of the World State and *World Constitution* for its Constitution. The lower house would be based in the UN General Assembly during the set-up period.

A democratic World State was called for by Truman, Einstein, Churchill, Eisenhower, Gandhi, Russell, J.F. Kennedy and Gorbachev, and I seem to be the only Western author/thinker continuing this tradition. The United Federation of the World would have limited supranational authority to bring in the seven goals (see above) and would create universal peace and prosperity within which existing nation-states and all humankind would thrive.

2. *My intentions*
My main intention is to spread awareness of the thinking behind the creation of a new World State in five different ways:

(1) Working with the UN by

- visiting António Guterres, who has already received the two books, and discussing how the UN General Assembly delegates can be involved in the planning of setting up a new World State; and
- giving a presentation to the UN General Assembly to lay my two books before the delegates so they can be sent back to their leaders, and to call for a Constitutional Convention to carry the idea forward.

Please note, Dr Roger Kotila, San-Francisco-based founder of the Center for United Nations Constitutional Research, has received the two books and has written that he wants me to meet Guterres and give a presentation to the UN General Assembly. He has taken the two books very seriously.

Government action needed: help in arranging a meeting with Guterres and setting up a presentation.

(2) Setting up a Foundation (Foundation for a United Federation of

the World, FUFW) in conjunction with a billionaire, to spread the idea and bring in the younger generation. See the list at the end for selected billionaires who have already received the two books. Also see the standard letter they have received.

Please note that Jeff Bezos has helped set up PeaceTech Accelerator which is housed in the US Institute of Peace (see *Sunday Times* article, https://www.thetimes.co.uk/article/what-amazon-boss-jeff-bezos-wants-for-christmas-is-world-peace-with-the-help-of-some-spies-and-special-forces-types-khjtk08k9/, two scanned pages attached) and that Michael Bloomberg's five criteria for philanthropic funding include "government innovation". (My initiative falls within this category.)

Government action needed: diplomatic contact with an appropriate billionaire to request assistance in setting up a Foundation.

(3) Giving a presentation to appropriate influential think tanks, e.g. London's Chatham House, Washington's Brookings Institution, and the Bilderberg Group.

Government action needed: arrange a platform for me to speak at Chatham House, Brookings Institute and the Bilderberg Group.

(4) Finding an international sponsor to buy a large quantity of the two books and get them sent to influential people, including the UN General Assembly delegates representing 193 nation-states.

Government action needed: help in identifying and contacting a sponsor and providing an appropriate list of recipients.

(5) Meeting key world leaders, beginning with appropriate leaders in the US, China, Russia and the EU, perhaps with the co-operation of Guterres, to discuss the new thinking.

Government action needed: help in getting me to key world leaders as I would be conveying a UK initiative.

3. The UK Government's position and perspective regarding the seven goals

The UK Government is in favour of the humanitarian thinking behind each of the seven goals. It:

- wants universal peace, has worked to stop the wars and terrorism, and has taken part in multilateral disarmament negotiations that have cut nuclear weapons from 69,401 nuclear weapons in 1985 to 14,900;
- aids disadvantaged humankind (e.g. by donating 0.7% of its national income a year for foreign aid);
- is engaged in solving environmental problems and global warming (e.g. it participated in the 2015 Paris Agreement);
- takes part in international programs to end disease and famine (e.g. British assistance in eradicating Ebola in Sierra Leone and famine in South Sudan);
- has supported solving the world's financial problems; and
- redistributes funds to the poorest of humankind (e.g. British aid to the refugee camps in Jordan and Lebanon).

All these actions/policies are aspects of British humanitarian values. All the international problems they address have been exacerbated by wars, which create refugees and require costly UK military involvement, and by the threat of nuclear weapons and need for appropriate defence expenditure.

From the UK's perspective, a limited federal and supranational strand to global governance would be worthwhile if it can bring solutions and cost-cutting in the areas of the seven goals and make for a better life for all humankind. It would be good if my innovative UK initiative could be included within Government thinking regarding the UK's post-Brexit global role.

4. The UK's post-Brexit global role

The UK's initiative in advancing this project will be well-regarded throughout the world as it will be a sign of global UK's caring for all humankind. The UK's image will be improved as it will be seen in caring, humanitarian rather than imperialistic terms, and may translate into new trade deals.

As the initiator of the idea, the UK will secure an advantageous place in the new world structure, see my emphasis on the position of Permanent Members of the UN/nuclear powers in relation to the allocation of members of the World Commission (see *World State*, p.176) and of seats in the World Senate (see *World State*, p.179).

It would be good if Government policy regarding the UK's post-Brexit global role could include exploring the feasibility of my innovative UK initiative.

5. Conservative Party's position and perspective

The Conservative Party defends the unitary UK's four nation-states and is strong on defence. It would welcome a multilateral universal peace and the resultant winding-down of defence expenditure which would bring a peace dividend that could be spent on increasing standards of living throughout the UK. While the idea is being projected and winning approval round the world, all present national arrangements would remain in place.

It could be that the global image of the UK can be improved *before* there is any change to the world's structure, and that the conveying of the initiative can in itself create a new perception of the UK's global role that can translate into increased trading benefits. It is important not to lose sight of the image-improving benefits of the initiative *before* its structure is implemented.

It would be good if exploring the feasibility of my innovative UK initiative could be adopted as a Conservative policy regarding the wider context of the UK's national life that can potentially win the assent of, and unite, Remainers and Leavers.

6. Ministerial/Prime-Ministerial support for my initiative

It would be good if this project could receive some UK Government support and assistance so it can be got across to the UN General Assembly and convey the UK's global mind-set.

It would also be good if the Prime Minister could refer to this project in a speech about the UK's post-Brexit global role at an appropriate time in 2018. I would be willing to help shape this speech. Prior to this eventuality, and preferably soon, a copy of this Résumé should be seen by the Prime Minister.

7. Summary of Government action proposed
To summarise, Government action could:

- get me to meet Guterres and address the UN General Assembly delegates to introduce the idea;
- help me set up a Foundation to spread the idea by persuading one of the billionaires to put in some funding;
- arrange a platform for me to speak at Chatham House, the Brookings Institute and the Bilderberg Group;
- help find a sponsor who would get books sent to influential people including the UN General Assembly delegates, and help compile a list of appropriate recipients;
- help me get to key world leaders; and
- arrange for the idea to be mentioned in a Prime-Ministerial speech on the UK's post-Brexit global role.

8. My position/title
It might help me advance the idea and open doors if I could be appointed an adviser/special adviser to the UK Government/Prime Minister on the UK's post-Brexit global role and/or a special envoy to the UN/world leaders on global restructuring.

Nicholas Hagger
www.nicholashagger.co.uk
27 December 2017; 3 January 2018

Appendix 2

Proposal to Set Up a
Supranational World Government (2022)

An approach to setting up a world government by the World Intellectual Forum based on Nicholas Hagger's *The World Government* (2010), *World State* (2018) and *World Constitution* (2018)

1. Objective

To create a democratic supranational world government with sufficient authority and legal powers to solve all the world's problems within seven areas, leaving all nation-states as they are internally and, except for the seven areas, internationally.

2. Why do we need a world government?

The international situation has become urgent following Russia's invasion of Ukraine and attack on the UN's post-1945 rules-based international order, and there is talk of a Third World War. The world has seemingly unsolvable problems that have impacted on all humankind:

1. wars and nuclear weapons (162 wars between 1945 and 2017 and around 40 ongoing wars in 2021, and 12,705 nuclear warheads in January 2022, around 2,000 of which are in active readiness including hypersonic intercontinental ballistic missiles that can destroy a country within three minutes), and seemingly no prospect of progress in voluntary disarmament;
2. shortage of resources and energy, poverty and hunger;
3. environmental problems such as global warming and famine;
4. self-perpetuating disease including the Covid pandemic;
5. lack of access to education, science and skills development;
6. an inadequate world economy and consequent financial and funding crises; and

7. a lack of spiritual and ethical awareness compounded by friction between religions that make wars more likely.

These problems are all interconnected, and to solve them would hugely benefit humankind as money could be diverted from spending on wars (that turn cities into rubble) and on nuclear weapons to building peaceful communities.

The UN, working at an international level with persuasion rather than at a supranational level with legal powers, does not have the legal authority to solve the world's problems. It needs a supranational 'add-on' to solve them within a democratic framework.

3. Can a new tier of cost and bureaucracy for a world government be justified?

Total global military expenditure was $2.113 trillion in 2022, and saving this amount annually by legally abolishing war, ending expenditure on arms and solving problem 1 would cover the cost of setting up a supranational world government that would solve all seven problems supranationally. Further funding would come from savings from solving problems 2 to 7, and phasing in the supranational world government gradually would stagger the cost.

The world government's solving all seven problems supranationally, which the UN with its international voluntary approach can never do, would justify its set-up cost and bureaucracy.

4. What will a world government do?

The world government will be confined to seven goals within seven communal areas:

1. Creating supranational legal powers to abolish and end war, keep a rules-based peace with human rights between nation-states with the aid of a world peace-keeping force, and achieve universal disarmament for the benefit of all humankind;
2. Sharing resources and energy supplies, and redistributing wealth

to eliminate poverty and hunger and to supply basic needs for the benefit of all humankind;

3. Solving environmental problems caused by climate change such as global warming and famine while respecting all life forms and avoiding violent farming methods, for the benefit of all humankind;

4. Ending disease, including eradicating Covid, and promoting wellness and good health in all for the benefit of all humankind;

5. Extending education, science and skills development for the benefit of all humankind;

6. Delivering a growing world economy and solving all financial and funding crises for the benefit of all humankind; and

7. Raising awareness of universal spirituality and global ethics, and ending all friction between religions so all religious leaders can co-operate, for the benefit of all humankind.

These problems are all interconnected, and solving one will be a contribution to solving the rest.

5. How will a world government differ from the system that already exists?

Nationalism is about humankind's differences in separate nation-states, and often leads to wars between nation-states. Internationalism is about the voluntary associations and relationships of nation-states, and the UN's restraining of separate nation-states.

Supranationalism is different because it unites all nation-states federally at the supranational level of the seven goals while nation-states continue to be separate internally and, apart from the seven communal areas of the seven goals, to be separate internationally. Nation-states, including the four main superpowers at present (the US, the EU, Russia and China), would agree to give up a little sovereignty in the areas of the seven goals in return for the huge benefit and cost-saving of having the world's problems solved in those seven areas.

A supranational world government would have legal powers to bring in the seven goals. At present the UN does not have these legal powers.

6. What will be the structure of a supranational world government?
Its structure is in the chart at the end (on p.183).

At the international level there would be a directly-elected democratic Lower House, a World Parliamentary Assembly, initially with 815 seats and eventually (when 26 currently dependent and 9 disputed territories can be represented) 850 seats. This would be a manageable size, not too large.

Initially the World Parliamentary Assembly could be housed in the UN General Assembly a few days a month as it is phased in. The UN Security Council would become a veto-less World Executive Council.

At the supranational level there would be a directly-elected Upper House, a World Senate with 92 senators in 46 zonal seats (2 per zonal seat); a World Commission which would operate like the European Commission; a World Council of Ministers with 29 World Departments; and a World President elected every four years.

The UN Secretary-General would be an important link between the international and supranational levels. The UN Secretary-General would oversee the World Parliamentary Assembly and report upwards to the World Senate's World Peace Enforcement Committee (see chart on p.183), which would in turn report upwards to the World Senate.

Over a period of time the UN General Assembly would be replaced by the World Parliamentary Assembly.

The structure would in total be that of a partly-federal, democratic World State, *partly* federal because it has just seven goals. The representatives of the legislative Lower House and senators of the Upper House would confine the World State's legal powers to the seven goals.

This is an ideal form of world government as it is a realistic and gradual process that takes account of the existing system. As a supranational 'add-on' with an important future link role for the UN Secretary-General, it may be acceptable to the UN as a basis for further study.

7. How would the supranational world government within the World State receive its legal powers?

The legal powers to set up the world government within a World State would be passed by the legislative Lower House, the World Parliamentary Assembly, and would be approved by the Upper House, the World Senate, and the World President in a democratic way.

The thinking behind this proposal includes the thinking in Clark and Sohn's *World Peace through World Law* (1958), which called for 17 revisions of the UN Charter so world law can enforce world peace.

8. In this approach, what would the World State be called?

In this model, the World State, a republic, would be called The United Federation of the World from a line in Tennyson's 'Locksley Hall' (1842): "In the Parliament of man, the Federation of the World." It would be known as the UF for short, an abbreviation that suggestively echoes the UN. The word 'United' suggestively incorporates the United States besides echoing the United Nations, and the word 'Federation' suggestively incorporates the Federation of Russia.

9. In this approach, what sources have been used?

This approach is based on Nicholas Hagger's *The World Government* (2010), *World State* (2018) and *World Constitution* (2018). In *The World Government* there are eight possible models for a world government. In *World State* the eighth model is presented as the ideal form for a World State. Both books have an extensive Bibliography.

There are 133 pages of detailed evidence and data in *World State*, including the world population figures of the nation-states as percentages of the world population based on the 2016 projections of the UN Department of Economic and Social Affairs. Seats in the World Parliamentary Assembly and World Senate, and membership of the World Commission, were allocated in accordance with the size of nation-states' populations and territories and their world influence. Adjustments were made for nuclear influence and Permanent Membership of the UN Security Council.

In *World Constitution* there are 145 articles in 14 chapters. A total of 26 constitutional precedents and 204 constitutions were consulted and are listed. They cover all aspects of a World State's rights, freedoms and structure.

10. Who has called for a World State in the past?

Plato's *Republic* presents an ideal city-state rather than a World State, but has much to say that chimes with setting up an ideal world government. Dante in *De Monarchia* (*On Monarchy*, sometimes translated as *On World Government*, c.1317–1318) wrote of "the whole Earth". Kant saw the need for an international state (*"civitas gentium"*) but wrote a "federation of free states" in *Perpetual Peace* (1795).

After 1945 and the atomic bomb there were calls for a world government by Truman (who kept Tennyson's line quoted in 8 above in his wallet), Einstein, Churchill, Eisenhower, Gandhi, Russell, J.F. Kennedy and Gorbachev, and many others.

11. What would a world with the seven goals implemented look like?

Our world with the seven goals achieved would look as follows:

1. War has been abolished, there is universal peace and universal disarmament has left the earth a safer place;
2. Resources have been shared, everyone has access to clean energy and a reasonable standard of living, all basic needs supplied, and poverty and hunger are no more;
3. Environmental problems and global warming have been coped with, and famine has been eliminated;
4. Everyone has a good standard of wellness and health, diseases have ended;
5. A good level of education, science and skill development is available everywhere and can be accessed by all;

6. The world economy is growing and there are no financial or funding crises; and

7. There is friendship between all religions, and all world citizens have a level of spirituality and approach life with attitudes that reflect global ethics, so crime is almost unknown.

As a result of the supranational World State, a Golden Age covers the earth. As under the *Pax Romana*, there have been no major wars for a long while, no cities pulverised to rubble, and civilisation has flourished.

12. What working groups are studying the feasibility of a supranational world government?

The World Intellectual Forum's global good governance working group, chaired by Nicholas Hagger and now under the umbrella of the World Intellectuals' Wisdom Forum, which is presenting this Proposal. Its terms of reference leave it open to other parallel proposals, not all of which will be as supranational or gradualist as this Proposal.

Arguably there should be a UN working group studying the feasibility of a supranational world government, and of all other kinds of world government, working in parallel with the World Intellectual Forum's working group.

13. What is the way forward for the World Intellectuals' Wisdom Forum working group?

World Intellectuals' Wisdom Forum is at present socialising this Proposal in Zoom calls to groups of interested individuals in Africa, China, the EU, India, Latin America, the Middle East, Pacific Asia, the UK and the US. Following further amendments to this Proposal a special website will be launched at a press conference to introduce the idea of a supranational world government and invite people to crowd-source input and ideas on a link for public input.

14. What next?

That will depend on the crowd-sourcing and public input. In this time of international urgency and concern at the talk of a Third World War and longing for all the leading nation-states to come together, the World Intellectuals' Wisdom Forum will be guided towards its next stage by public opinion.

Relevant details on Nicholas Hagger

Nicholas Hagger is a British poet, man of letters, cultural historian and philosopher. He read Law and then English Literature at Oxford University and has lectured at universities in Iraq, Libya and Japan, where he was a Professor of English Literature. Following a 30-year-long Mystic Way, in the course of which he experienced full illumination and enlightenment, he found he had instinctive unitive vision, which sees unity behind all apparent differences and all academic disciplines. His philosophy of Universalism presents the fundamental unity of the universe and all humankind. He is the author of 60 books, and his Universalist approach can be found in each. It has been said that he is at home in many disciplines, like a Renaissance man.

He is a Gusi Peace Prize Laureate for Literature, and has a BRICS silver medal for 'Vision for Future'. His archive is held at the University of Essex, UK, where in May 2019 there was an exhibition about his works that displayed manuscripts relating to *World State* and *World Constitution*. His website is www.nicholashagger.co.uk.

30 July 2022

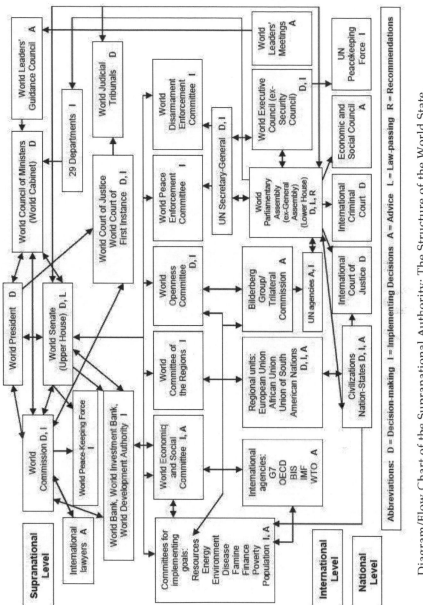

Diagram/Flow Chart of the Supranational Authority: The Structure of the World State.

Abbreviations: D = Decision-making I = Implementing Decisions A = Advice L = Law-passing R = Recommendations

Notes and References to Sources
within *The Golden Phoenix*

Preface
Russia, Ukraine, a Supranational 'Golden Phoenix' New World Order
and a Coming Golden Age
1. Nicholas Hagger, *The Fall of the West*, pp.26–27.

1. Russia: Inaugurating a New Age and World Empire
1. Hagger, *The Fall of the West*, pp.7, 74.
2. Hagger, *The Fall of the West*, p.4.
3. Hagger, *The Syndicate*, pp.23–25, see also *The Fall of the West*, pp.4–5.
4. Hagger, *Peace for our Time*, p.8.
5. Hagger, *Peace for our Time*, pp.40–50.
6. Hagger, *Peace for our Time*, pp.37–38.
7. Hagger, *Peace for our Time*, p.39.
8. Hagger, *Peace for our Time*, pp.107–110.
9. Hagger, *Peace for our Time*, p.117.
10. Hagger, *Peace for our Time*, pp.173–186.
11. Hagger, *Peace for our Time*, pp.202–207.
12. Hagger, *Peace for our Time*, p.217.
13. Hagger, *Peace for our Time*, pp.201–221.
14. Hagger, *Peace for our Time*, p.201.
15. Hagger, *My Double Life 2: A Rainbow over the Hills*, pp.523–524.
16. Hagger, *My Double Life 2: A Rainbow over the Hills*, pp.530–534.
17. See https://peaceman.ru/materialseng.
18. Hagger, *Collected Poems 1958–2006*, pp.93–94.

2. Ukraine: Why Russia's Invasion of Ukraine Happened, and
   a New Russian World Order
1. Hagger, *The Fall of the West*, p.6; Hagger, *The Syndicate*, p.22.
2. Hagger, *The Fall of the West*, p.6.
3. Hagger, *The Fall of the West*, p.25.

4. Hagger, *The Fall of the West*, p.25; Frederic Morton, *The Rothschilds: A Family Portrait*, pp.150–152.

5. Hagger, *The Fall of the West*, p.25; *Spotlight*, 22 April 1996, pp.4–5.

6. Hagger, *The Fall of the West*, p.25; Hagger, *The Secret American Dream*, pp.129–130.

7. See 'Gazprom OAO history, profile and corporate video', see https://www.companieshistory.com/gazprom/.

8. Hagger, *The Fall of the West*, p.25.

9. Hagger, *The Fall of the West*, p.25; Hagger, *The Secret American Dream*, pp.145–148.

10. Hagger, *The Fall of the West*, p.26.

11. Hagger, *The Fall of the West*, p.27.

12. Rupert Russell, *Price Wars*.

13. Hagger, *The Fall of the West*, p.31.

14. Hagger, *The Fall of the West*, pp.31–32.

15. Lex Fridman interview with Oliver Stone, who interviewed Putin between 2014 and 2016, in Mercola, 'Is there a way out of the Russia-Ukraine War?', see https://noqreport.com/2022/06/03/oliver-stone-is-there-a-way-out-of-the-russia-ukraine-war/.

16. Putin's full 'Empire of Lies' speech from Thursday 24 February 2022 on Russia's invasion of Ukraine, see https://www.aljazeera.com/news/2022/2/24/putins-speech-declaring-war-on-ukraine-translated-excerpts.

17. Lex Fridman interview with Oliver Stone, in Mercola, 'Is there a way out of the Russia-Ukraine War?', see https://noqreport.com/2022/06/03/oliver-stone-is-there-a-way-out-of-the-russia-ukraine-war/.

18. *Tass*, release of news bulletin, 9 March 2022, 'Russian Defense Ministry publishes Kiev's secret order for offensive against Donbass', see https://tass.com/politics/1418861.

19. 'Kiev's Secret Order for a March Offensive Against Donbass?', see https://www.globalresearch.ca/breaking-russian-defense-ministry-publishes-kievs-secret-order-offensive-against-don bass/5773652.

20. Lex Fridman interview with Oliver Stone, in Mercola, 'Is there a way out of the Russia-Ukraine War?', see https://noqreport.com/2022/06/03/oliver-stone-is-there-a-way-out-of-the-russia-ukraine-war/.

21. 'Ukraine crisis is about Great Power oil, gas pipeline rivalry', see https://www.theguardian.com/environment/earth-insight/2014/mar/06/ukraine-crisis-great-power-oil-gas-rivals-pipelines.

22. Glenn Greenwald, 'Biden Wanted $33B More For Ukraine. Congress Quickly Raised it to $40B. Who Benefits?', see https://scheerpost.com/2022/05/11/greenwald-biden-wanted-33b-more-for-ukraine-congress-quickly-raised-it-to-40b-who-benefits/.

23. Hagger, *The Fall of the West*, pp.84–86.

24. Nuland: 'Ukraine has "Biological Research Facilities", Russian MoD responds at UN Security Council', see https://www.europereloaded.com/victoria-nuland-ukraine-has-biological-research-facilities-russian-mod-responds/.

25. Nuland: 'Ukraine has "Biological Research Facilities", Russian MoD responds at UN Security Council', see https://www.europereloaded.com/victoria-nuland-ukraine-has-biological-research-facilities-russian-mod-responds/.

26. Hagger, *The Fall of the West*, p.73.

27. 'Statement by Permanent Representative Vassily Nebenzia at UNSC briefing on biological laboratories in Ukraine', see https://www.europereloaded.com/victoria-nuland-ukraine-has-biological-research-facilities-russian-mod-responds/; and https://www.un.org/press/en/2022/sc14827.doc.htm.

28. See https://www.europereloaded.com/victoria-nuland-ukraine-has-biological-research-facilities-russian-mod-responds/.

29. 'Briefing on the results of the analysis of documents related to the military biological activities of the United States on the territory of Ukraine', see https://eng.mil.ru/en/special_operation/news/more.htm?id=12420908@egNews.

30. 'Russia Is Lying About Evidence of Bioweapons Labs in Ukraine, Russian Biologists Say', see https://theintercept.com/2022/03/17/russia-ukraine-bioweapons-misinformation/.

31. See https://fij.ng/article/putin-preparing-ukraines-ex-president-yanukovych-for-zelenskys-job/.

32. 'U.S. says China and Russia seek "profoundly illiberal" world order', see https://www.taiwannews.com.tw/en/news/4453506.

33. See https://www.independent.co.uk/news/world/americas/us-

politics/new-world-order-meaning-biden-b2043111.html.

34. 'Putin compares himself to Peter the Great in quest to take back Russian lands', see https://www.theguardian.com/world/2022/jun/10/putin-compares-himself-to-peter-the-great-in-quest-to-take-back-russian-lands; also see *The Times*, 10 June 2022, 'I'm reconquering just like Peter the Great, insists Putin'; and *The Daily Telegraph*, 10 June 2022, 'President likens himself to Peter the Great as he "reclaims" land for Russia'.

35. 'Putin compares himself to Peter the Great in quest to take back Russian lands', see https://www.theguardian.com/world/2022/jun/10/putin-compares-himself-to-peter-the-great-in-quest-to-take-back-russian-lands.

36. *The Times*, 11 June 2022, 'Nursery children sing in praise of "Uncle Vlad"', see https://www.thetimes.co.uk/article/schoolchildren-sing-in-praise-of-putin-vjt55gfhk.

37. 'Russia's former president Dmitry Medvedev says the West is risking "fully fledged nuclear war" between Moscow and NATO by "pumping weapons into Ukraine"', see https://www.dailymail.co.uk/news/article-10809339/Russias-former-President-Medvedev-warns-Western-military-aid-Ukraine-risks-sparking-nuclear-war.html.

38. See https://www.lbc.co.uk/news/russia-threatens-uk-nuclear-satan-2-hypersonic-missile/. Also see https://www.wlrfm.com/news/russian-tv-clip-shows-nuclear-bomb-being-dropped-on-ireland-248315.

39. Hagger, *The Fall of the West*, pp.120–121.

40. Hagger, *The Fall of the West*, pp.124–125.

41. Hagger, *The Fall of the West*, p.85.

42. Joseph Mercola, 'Patents prove SARS-CoV-2 is a manufactured virus', https://www.organicconsumers.org/news/patents-prove-sars-cov-2-manufactured-virus.

43. Joseph Mercola, 'Will 100 million die from the Covid vax by 2028?'.

44. Hagger, *The Fall of the West*, pp.85–86.

45. Hagger, *The Fall of the West*, pp.60, 84–88.

46. Hagger, *The Fall of the West*, pp.xxiv, 73, 89.

47. 'Gazprom to quit supplying the largest Dutch gas trader', see

https://dutchreview.com/new/gazprom-to-stop-supplying-gas-to-dutch-gas-company-starting-today/.

48. Hagger, *The Fall of the West*, pp.101–107.
49. Hagger, *The Fall of the West*, p.106.
50. Hagger, *The Fall of the West*, p.127, see https://covid-unmasked.net/agenda-21-year-2021-depopulation-sustainable-development-humans-this-could-form-a-website-in-itself-ed/.
51. 'Russian President Vladimir Putin meets with World Economic Forum Chairman Klaus Schwab', see https://www.weforum.org/agenda/2022/05/davos-2022-klaus-schwab-trust-based-and-action-oriented-cooperation/; also see https://forumspb.com/en/news/news/russian-president-vladimir-putin-meets-with-world-economic-forum-chairman-klaus-schwab/.
52. See https://www.weforum.org/agenda/2022/05/davos-2022-klaus-schwab-trust-based-and-action-oriented-cooperation/.

3. What Happens Next: A Third World War or a Further Fall of the West, a Coming New World Order

1. Timothy Snyder, *The Road to Unfreedom*, pp.16–18, 29–30.
2. Snyder, *op. cit.*, pp.63–64.
3. *The Sunday Telegraph*, 12 June 2022, James Crisp, 'The West must supply Ukraine with weapons for "as long as it takes", Latvia says', https://www.telegraph.co.uk/world-news/2022/06/12/west-must-supply-ukraine-weapons-long-takes-latvia-says/ (subscription to *The Telegraph* needed to read the article online).
4. *The Sunday Telegraph*, 12 June 2022, James Crisp, 'The West must supply Ukraine with weapons for "as long as it takes", Latvia says', https://www.telegraph.co.uk/world-news/2022/06/12/west-must-supply-ukraine-weapons-long-takes-latvia-says/ (subscription to *The Telegraph* needed to read the article online).
5. *MailOnline*, 16 June 2022, 'Huge fire breaks out at Russia's largest gas field as pipe bursts, threatening supplies to Europe', https://www.dailymail.co.uk/news/article-10923271/Huge-fire-breaks-Russias-largest-gas-field-pipe-bursts.html.
6. 'World War Three "a real danger"', says Russian foreign minister

Sergei Lavrov', https://www.standard.co.uk/news/world/world-war-three-danger-sergey-lavrov-russia-ukraine-b996251.html.

7. *Sunday Times Magazine*, pp.28–41, see http://www.judecollins.com/2022/06/henry-kissinger-at-99-by-donal-kennedy/.

8. Hagger, *The Syndicate*, p.120; and *The Fall of the West*, p.10.

9. Hagger, *The Fall of the West*, pp.xii, 39, 109, 111.

10. Hagger, *The Fall of the West*, pp.41–42.

11. Hagger, *My Double Life 2: A Rainbow over the Hills*, p.502.

12. Hagger, *The Fall of the West*, pp.128–135.

13. Hagger, *The Fall of the West*, pp.107, 109.

14. Hagger, *The Fall of the West*, pp.95–97.

15. Hagger, *The Fall of the West*, pp.77–82.

16. Hagger, *The Fall of the West*, pp.xix, xxiv–xxv, 142–143, 172; and *My Double Life 1: This Dark Wood*, pp.196–200, 505–516.

17. Hagger, *The Syndicate*, pp.10–12; and *The Fall of the West*, p.45.

18. Hagger, *The Fall of the West*, p.48.

19. Hagger, *The Fall of the West*, pp.26–27.

20. Hagger, *The Fall of the West*, p.10.

21. Hagger, *The Fall of the West*, p.48.

22. Hagger, *The Fall of the West*, p.45.

23. Jeffrey D. Sachs, 'The West's False Narrative about Russia and China', 22 August 2022, https://www.jeffsachs.org/newspaper-articles/h29g9k7l7fymxp39yhzwxc5f72ancr.

24. Hagger, *The Fall of the West*, pp.120–121.

25. See https://sdg.iisd.org/commentary/guest-articles/the-2022-global-peoples-assembly-and-a-new-multilateralism/#:~:text=In%20an%208%20September%202022,take%20place%20until%20September%202024.

26. See https://www.voltairenet.org/article218334.html.

Bibliography

Hagger, Nicholas, *Collected Poems 1958–2006*, O-Books, 2006.

Hagger, Nicholas, *Fools' Gold*, O-Books, 2022.

Hagger, Nicholas, *King Charles the Wise*, O-Books, 2018.

Hagger, Nicholas, *My Double Life 1: This Dark Wood*, O-Books, 2015.

Hagger, Nicholas, *My Double Life 2: A Rainbow over the Hills*, O-Books, 2015.

Hagger, Nicholas, *Overlord*, O-Books, 2006.

Hagger, Nicholas, *Peace for our Time*, O-Books, 2018.

Hagger, Nicholas, *The Algorithm of Creation*, O-Books, 2023.

Hagger, Nicholas, *The Fall of the West*, O-Books, 2022.

Hagger, Nicholas, *The Fire and the Stones*, Element, 1991.

Hagger, Nicholas, *The New Philosophy of Universalism*, O-Books, 2009.

Hagger, Nicholas, *The Promised Land*, O-Books, 2023.

Hagger, Nicholas, *The Rise and Fall of Civilizations*, O-Books, 2008.

Hagger, Nicholas, *The Secret American Dream*, Watkins, 2011.

Hagger, Nicholas, *The Secret History of the West*, O-Books, 2005.

Hagger, Nicholas, *The Syndicate*, O-Books, 2004.

Hagger, Nicholas, *The World Government*, O-Books, 2010.

Hagger, Nicholas, *World Constitution*, O-Books, 2018.

Hagger, Nicholas, *World State*, O-Books, 2018.

Morton, Frederic, *The Rothschilds: A Family Portrait*, Atheneum, New York, 1962.

Russell, Rupert, *Price Wars*, Doubleday Books, 2022.

Snyder, Timothy, *The Road to Unfreedom*, Vintage, 2018.

Index

O-BOOKS

O is a symbol of the world, of oneness and unity; this eye represents knowledge and insight. We publish titles on general spirituality and living a spiritual life. We aim to inform and help you on your own journey in this life.
If you have enjoyed this book, why not tell other readers by posting a review on your preferred book site?